How to Win Her & Influence Him

The Ultimate Guide to Understanding & Fixing Relationship Problems

Genie Goodwin

To the Love of my life, the man of my dreams, Michael.
Thank you for a lifetime of love, our own legendary love affair.

Acknowledgments

I am extraordinarily blessed to have the love, support and skill of the following people without whom this book would not exist. To Michael, my husband, the man of my dreams who has supported my dreams unwaveringly, no matter how outrageous they seemed. To Marisa, Shane & Bree, my amazing children who've taught me more about walking in love than I could ever have imagined. To Citajean Lawrence, and Teresa Moore, my beautiful, brilliant, creative, and loving sisters who never settle, nor allow me to settle. To Deanna Maio, Anita Kirkman, & Helen Hunter, thank you for your constant encouragement to reach for the stars and change the world. To Robert Moore, Buck Lawrence, Paul Drexel & Jeana Watts, & Kate at Aevum Images, your help and compassion are deeply appreciated. To Shane Goodwin, your design skills rock my world.

Table of Contents

Foreword

As the CEO of a $300 million company, it looked like I had it all, it appeared as if I was a successful man. I didn't do it by myself, no one does. It took hard work and a lot of people to do it, and I loved it. One of the core concepts I understood was: it takes high performing people and healthy relationships to build a successful business. Even then, I was on many different medications, my wife and children rarely saw me, and when they did I was exhausted. It didn't feel successful to me.

Many leaders in business have this experience. It appears they have it all; it looks like they are successful, but in practice it is an empty, draining, lonely existence of unending hard work. That's wrong. I learned a hard lesson, yet a core piece of wisdom to experiencing a profitable business and a fulfilling life: in order to teach, train and equip others towards sustainable transformation in their organizations, I first had to transform my own personal life at home. Because there is no fulfillment without a successful home life.

I had to make the transition into a deeper level of relationship at home, and I couldn't do that without removing my own personal constraints (of which I had many). I had to deal with my own limitations before I could attempt to create better, more open relationships at home.   Once I began that process I could then use that wisdom to transform companies and other organizations. That's what we do now at The FSH Group.   Through a combination of leadership training and strategic consulting, we are building a better world, one person, one family, and one company at a time.

It is personal constraints that hold back the experience of success as a leader.   The more free you are of these, the more fulfillment you can experience both personally and organizationally.   It's a marriage of the business transactional mind with the relational mind where I found true success.

In **How to Win Her & Influence Him**, Genie Goodwin relates the transactional vs relational concepts to male/female dynamics.   Generally, the male focus is like the business mind: "get 'er done," achieve, solve. By and large, the female focus is similar to the relationship mind: create community, make sure everyone feels included, involved and connected in the work.   Although, as Genie reveals, we are all unique, and men can be relational while women can be transactional.   It's in understanding the differences and how to work with men and women that we can create healthier, stronger relationships to fuel our success.

Ms. Goodwin is bright and bold, but most importantly, committed to walking in love; a dangerous (in a very good way) combination.   She walks her talk.   Her authenticity is immediately evident and her passion is contagious.   She learned what she knows about relationships as a necessity, by making her own mistakes in her relationships and by being committed to saving them by walking in love. That is her standard and her commitment.

Genie is a master communicator at unveiling clear, practical, actionable strategies that will help you create deeper, richer, more fulfilling relationships that fuel genuine success. Her wisdom and understanding is in helping people and organizations build relationships that can outlast any challenges that come their way. She has devoted her life to studying men and women, how they work, what motivates them, and how to help them grow. From this devotion she has honed a skill that can look at a relationship, diagnose the piece that is causing devastation and wipe it out.

In **How to Win Her & Influence Him** she'll share with you the secrets to getting past the offense, the mis-understanding, the conflict that comes in all relationships. You'll learn the reasons men act the way they do and how to work better with them. You'll also learn, why women act the way they do and how to serve them better so each of us can get the love we want and experience abiding success at home that fuels our success at work.

I am honored, humbled and grateful to be a part of this work and eager to see the change we can enact together, when each of us learns the secrets to walking in love. You're about to meet an amazing teacher named Genie

Goodwin and go on a journey that will truly be life changing. Enjoy the ride.

-Ford Taylor,

Founder FSH Group/Transformational Leadership

Introduction

In The Beginning...

I was stunned, I couldn't speak, I couldn't breathe and I couldn't stop smiling.   I wasn't known for ever having a lack of words but... could this be true? Was this real?

I was lying on a grassy hill in the park on a beautiful late summer evening as I gazed up at the blanket of stars twinkling above me.   I beamed with a joy that couldn't be contained...it felt like it would burst out of my chest.

He leaned over me with shining hazel eyes, brighter than the stars and said, "Will you always smile like that for me?"

All I could say was, "You put it there!"   His response was a passionate kiss.

The most handsome man I had ever met had just asked me to marry him.   I was so happy I couldn't even answer him...but the answer was written all over my face.

There was no way to know just four short weeks earlier, standing in line at the Department of Motor Vehicles, my whole life was about to change. This tall, dark and handsome man had entered my life and my world spun. He was at least a dozen people ahead of me in line as we waited to take care of our business. I glanced his way and noticed deep hazel eyes locked on me. My hands started shaking, my knees went weak, my eyes darted away before he could see his effect on me. I had never experienced anything like this before but it was too late, I was caught. It was as if my body, my heart sang just for him. It felt like something in me recognized something in him, something I would find I wasn't willing to live without.

That was the beginning of the rest of my life. It only took him one month to propose.

In that month it was as if my whole world realigned to revolve around him. Suddenly I couldn't imagine living without him. How had he entwined himself with my every breath? This stranger, this man inserted himself into my life and suddenly I was willing to give up everything I knew and follow him anywhere on the planet. At first it made me angry, I was so young and now it was all about him, but I was in love and I had it bad.

I had found the secret to life: There is no life without love.

The End Of The Beginning....

But there is something about love that I was about to discover that I want to share with you.

It took me two years with the man of my dreams to go from madly in love to --- just plain mad...angry...frustrated. Where was that man who made my hands shake? Now he made my fists shake. Where was the man who made my knees go weak? Now it seemed like his callousness brought me to my knees. Where was the attention, the romance, the conversation?

Where did the love go while we weren't looking?

Why do people change after the wedding? He seems distant though he started out in hot pursuit, making sure she had anything she wanted. She seems fussy, complains constantly, though she started out happy and easily pleased. It seems like love is fickle, it comes and goes almost on a whim. We start out madly in love and then end up just mad.

What is it about love that makes it so hard to stay in love? How do I fall in love without losing it along the way? Are there things we can do to keep love alive, burning brighter than ever before or even bring it back from the dead?

Yes. (A resounding yes!)

That's what you are about to delve into. I've learned the ultimate secret to bringing love back from the dead and everything in between.

How To Read This Book

The first half of this book, Chapter 1 through Chapter 6 is written for him. So that he may uncover the secrets to winning her for himself. Every man wants to win his own Beauty for his own castle. If he really wants to understand her, I suggest he keep reading into the second half of the book, to see life from her perspective. Ladies, I highly recommend you read the first half written to men. It is written through their perspective of what they experience in a relationship with women, try not to judge them but rather reach for understanding.

The second half, from chapter 7 through Chapter 12 is for her. Every woman wants to influence her man, be an integral part of his life. So that she may discover the true and most beautiful ways to influence her man and bring out the hero, the knight in shining armor who daily lays down his life to adore her.

The final chapter is a sneak preview to help both of you with the male/female dynamics that show up at work, making work harder than it has to be. So you may create compelling and profitable relationships at work and avoid the stress of war of the sexes at work.

Whenever you come upon this icon: Pay close attention. This marks the miraculous strategies, words and actions that can transform situations. I've set them apart for you so you can use the book as an interactive guide. When you run into challenging situations, if you want INSTANT RESULTS look for the genie icon. You can look up the chapter that applies to what you are experiencing and simply locate the icon and follow the instructions exactly.

There are lots of opportunities for you to go deeper in the content, gain access to several free training videos, participate in some interactive livecast events and register to get updates to this book as it gets expanded and I correct the inevitable errors, grammar and spelling mistakes we've tried hard to avoid, but may be here.

In fact, if you find any mistakes, PLEASE tell me by sending the error and location you found it on to my email: support@livesuccessnow.com. Thank you in advance for your help.

Finally, as I refer to men and women and the differences between the sexes, I'm referring to male/female dynamics, the brain science between the sexes, as well as preferences between masculine and feminine energies. Because men can walk in feminine energy and women can walk in masculine energy, you may find as you read this book that descriptions of thoughts, feelings and actions don't seem to apply to you in every circumstance, or situation. This is normal. Most of us can shift between masculine and feminine energy throughout the day depending upon what we are dealing with but this does not affect our core energy, nor does it affect the amazing reactions we have when our needs are met in the way we can receive them.

May your journey into **How to Win Her & Influence Him**, be your wake-up call to the many ways you can get the love you want, whenever you want it, no matter what you are going through if you simply learn the secrets to walking in love.

Chapter One for Men
Win Her Heart:
How Can I Make Her Happy?

There's something about a woman, maybe it's the shine of her hair, the impossible softness of her skin, the playful look in her eye, the curve of her hips, or that glorious, radiant smile that catches your breath.   Just looking at her makes you feel good and you want more. Being with her lights up your life and awakens an ache in you that demands to be satisfied.

When a man loves a woman, he can't keep his mind on nothing else

He'll trade the world for the good thing he's found

If she is bad, he can't see it, she can do no wrong

Turn his back on his best friend if he put her down

When a man loves

a woman, spend his very last dime

Tryin' to hold on to what he needs

He'd give up all his comforts, sleep out in the rain

If she said that's the way it ought to be

-When a Man Loves a Woman,
Percy Sledge

Do you remember how it felt when you first saw her?

Do you remember how it felt when you first touched her?

Do you remember how it felt when you knew she was the one?

Let the pursuit begin. You would do, say, give, anything to win her. I once heard a preacher say, "I was prepared to lie, to say anything to make her marry me, then I'd make it up to her later!"

You meet her, set your sights on her and set out to win her.

When you set out to win a woman, the flowers start flowing, candle lit dinners, chocolates, poems, dancing in the moonlight, long walks with long conversations, holding hands, opening doors, buying presents, finding adventures to share, and date after date after date. It's magnificent. When she smiles at you there is a fullness in your life, as if you were a better man just because she is with you.

Then the most amazing thing kicks in...an intense desire to provide for her, to protect her and make her your own so that you can spend your life caring for her. When you provide for her, when what you do makes her happy and you see that smile, the reward filling your chest is almost more than you can bear. You wonder how you got so blessed.

It is a wonder. It is love and it is the ultimate thing in life. The thing that makes life worth living. It makes the long hard days worth it. There is no mountain too high, no valley too deep, no challenge too hard, because your life sings with a reason—love.

Love makes heroes out of men. When a woman finds a hero that's all hers, she will follow him anywhere on the planet and she will blossom into The Beauty. Love makes each of us better than we can ever be without it.

And then... we lose it. Sometimes it's fast, sometimes it's a slow drain...but no matter how much you love, we all go through it as if it's some part of a mysterious plan.

I'm Crazy In Love With Her But She Drives Me Crazy!

"I am crazy in love with my wife, and she drives me crazy! I'm not sure what happened, but as the years rolled by there seemed to be less and less room for me in her life. I was too messy in the living room, so the sofa got covered with plastic. I left too many things in the den, I got organized right out of it. Her closet in the bedroom got bigger and bigger and mine got smaller and smaller. Her attention was for the kids and she was too tired for me. I still love my wife but I find my comfort elsewhere. I don't know when I lost her and I'm scared, because now I think I want someone else."

This was one of my clients. He still loved his wife but he had no place in her life and without realizing it, in an attempt to please her, he moved himself out of her life room by room until he found his comfort and space elsewhere. That's where he lost her and she lost him because no matter what he did, she was not pleased. This is typically where I hear: "we just grew apart" or "I must have married the wrong person" or "it's just too hard and nothing works."

This couple ran into the #1 problem we all run into when we are trying to love. In fact, I tell my clients that the reason for the majority of the fights, heart-break, lonely nights, snarky words, even divorce... all of the ugly things we do to the ones we love is this: men love women as if they were men. Conversely, women love men as if they were women. But men don't want what women want; and women certainly don't want what men want. When you keep giving someone something they don't want (even though you call it love) they eventually don't want you and they think you don't want them.

Here it is, the ultimate secret: love is ALWAYS the answer, no matter the challenge, because love is the most powerful force on the planet and love is something we can't live without. That's why even though we have our hearts broken into millions of pieces we will tie the pieces together and try to find love with someone else.

As I reveal this ultimate truth to you, I'll unveil what love is to a woman (How to Win Her) and what love is to a man (How to Influence Him) so you will have the ultimate answer to love without losing it in as many situations as I can fit in this book.

I Won Her Heart - What Happened?

The problems began with the idea that once you've won her heart and the COMMITMENT IS MADE, the battle is over and you've brought home your prize. No more winning is required, she's all yours. Then all of your attention shifts to providing for and protecting your prize. So you work. You work hard because of how much you love her and how much you want to provide for her. When you come home you have nothing left to give, you just want to bask in the reward of her love for all of your hard work.

You walk in the door after a long day, go through your unwinding ritual, about twenty minutes later you go looking for your woman. But the strangest thing has happened, she is upset at you and you have no idea why. Where's your reward for all your hard work? Your reward is not waiting for you, what's waiting for you is more work (take out the trash, pick up your socks, did you bring home the groceries I needed?), or worse, she wants you to talk all about your day with her. That's the last thing you want! You want to forget about work and the battles of the day, you want your reward: her and her attention and appreciation for all you've already done.

This repeats itself day after day, draining away the love. You begin to feel used, unappreciated, unwanted. Here's the first problem, while most people know love is alive and it takes constant attention; most men do not know the heart of a woman is **not** something you can win once and walk away from, thinking you'll always have it. That's akin to thinking you'll be satisfied with having sex once and it's enough for the rest of your life. A woman's heart requires constant attention from her man. That's why when your attention turns from winning her, to providing for her, she feels as if she's lost you.

How Do I Hang On To The Win?

The way to a woman's heart is attention, C O N S T A N T and never-ending attention, but it's not the kind of attention you think it is. A woman's favorite way of getting attention is through a conversation filled with details. The longer the conversation, the more the details, the happier she is. That's why when you come home from work she wants to talk and talk and talk. This is her cry for connection with you. It means she's missed you and wants to be a part of all you've done while you were apart. When you don't want to talk about your day it's as if something switches in her brain and she thinks: you don't love her, or you are hiding something from her. Seriously, she thinks you might be lying to her because you don't talk to her like a woman would with lots and lots of details about your day.

This repeats itself day after day: she thinks you no longer love her, you no longer want her, and you are hiding something from her. You can see it show up when she starts questioning you like a lawyer; when she starts trying to fix everything around the house, including you and when she complains constantly.

Believe it or not, the answer isn't to move out in order to please her. This will not make her happy, because she doesn't actually want less of you. When you move out in order to please her it's the beginning stage of growing apart. More importantly, when you leave in order to get peace for yourself and to give her peace to find her own answers, she believes you have abandoned her in her time of need. This further contributes to the growing apart syndrome. Because now she must go find someone else to feel close to as she works through the issues in her life. Remember, what you need (peace and quiet) is not what she needs. It's important that you discover what she needs and give that to her.

Come a Little Closer

There's a great reason for her actions and it is not what you think...you see, when a woman wants another woman to change something, she complains. Women know that complaining is simply a request to change so you can be closer. Therefore, when a woman hears a complaint she makes a change to come closer. She doesn't receive it as you do: there is something wrong with you. Frankly, all women think there is something wrong with them, therefore it's not an issue when someone brings it up. Change is an opportunity to get better and to get closer. Women have an innate drive to get closer, to create intimacy and they are in a constant battle with the thoughts that they need to be better, to be more.   Women do not see themselves as the magnificent creature you do.   Let me be clear: women use complaining to get closer and they do not understand why it doesn't work on men.

Remember that what makes you happy will not make her happy.   What that means is, be aware of what she really wants when she's complaining: TO GET CLOSER TO YOU.   It's not about the room she's complaining about so much as the feeling she gets that you care for her and what she's going through in that room.   She's not really asking you to leave the living room to make her happy, she's asking you to show appreciation for what she's going through.   Honor her daily battles the way you want to be honored for yours- simply express gratitude for all she does as she complains, and stay in the room!

How Can I Make Her Happy?

You can win her every day through her favorite form of attention: conversation.   Think about it, that's exactly how you won her in the first place, through attentive conversation.   I challenge you to set a timer for 10 minutes.   Tell her you want to hear all about her day. Then give her ten solid minutes of your complete and focused attention listening to her.   WARNING: DO NOT try to fix anything she says or is going through. (We'll talk about fixing in Chapter 5).   The key to this is your **focused presence** while listening to her.   Try to feel what she's feeling simply for the purpose of being with her. This will daily win the heart of your woman. If you are brilliant, you will give her more time as you find the magnificent rewards that come from listening to your woman: she will blossom right before your eyes. That's the glorious gift your love brings to her.

For extra points, when you notice more complaints, do these things: Text her at least once a day and tell her you miss her touch, or her laugh, or her smile. Call her at least once a day and tell her you were thinking about her and needed to hear her voice even though you only had a minute to talk. Look for things you both can enjoy together and make time for them at least once a week. Talk, laugh, play, love...it seems so simple but someone once said, if it's simple to do, it's simple to forget. Don't forget, schedule it on your calendar to remind yourself every day.

Want more?

Go to:

http://www.livesuccessnow.com/more-win-influence/

for training taking you even deeper.

Chapter Two for Men
Win Her Soul:
How Do I Handle Her When She's Upset?

"I came home from a long, hard day and she was upset. She was not happy to see me; she was not happy, period. The kids were running around, dinner was not ready and she looked like she's been pulled through a keyhole. Why can't dinner be ready? She's got all day to herself. What's so hard about cleaning a house? I constantly tell her how to do it better but she just doesn't do it. It's like she wants to be unhappy. This isn't hard, she just won't do it. When I bring it up she argues, defends, gets upset and then pulls away from me as if I was somehow the problem; sometimes she cries and then it takes days for her to get over it. The answer is so easy. I don't understand why she can't take instruction. Why does she take it personally? I have no idea how to talk to her when she's upset so we can just get through it."

This was another of my clients. He loved his wife, but every night seemed like a battleground when he got home, not the bastion of peace he longed for. He assumed he knew why she was upset so he did his best to help her by giving her more efficient ways to get things done so she wouldn't be upset. It looked so easy to him, but the more he instructed her, the colder she got and the more she pulled away. To him it seemed like she purposely made things complicated so she could then get upset about them, instead of just fixing them. Once she got upset, it appeared that nothing he did could make it better. He would then retreat: spend time in the yard, in the garage, or more hours at work. In a few days she would seem to get over it; but they couldn't ever seem to get back to loving each other and enjoying each other's company. It was as if they were doomed to stay miserable together.

I affectionately call this the "Successfully Miserable" stage. Because you've worked hard to win her, now you work hard to provide for her. It takes work to maintain all you provide for her but it seems like she refuses to be happy, no matter what you provide or do. Then once she gets upset, you are clueless as to why she's upset and even more lost as to what to do about it. So you retreat until she gets over it, which may take days; until the next senseless battle begins and the whole thing repeats itself.

We've run into a major characteristic about men (that women don't know about) and conversely a major characteristic about women (that men don't know about) that causes massive damage to our relationships.

How to Make an Upset Woman Even More Upset!

As a men you are the fixers of the universe. This is what you are here for. You are the hero who gets things done, preferably as efficiently as possible. You pour the fuel of your life into providing solutions for others and you are magnificent at it. Your brain processes the quickest, most efficient solutions and offer them up as swiftly and effectively as possible.[1] That means since you have calculated the solution you don't need to hear the rest of the problem. That would just waste precious time. So you cut her off and tell her how to solve the problem. Because the quicker the fix the better; and if she's talking about it without offering the fix it must mean she needs you to fix it. Every man knows: if it's not broken, don't waste your energy trying to fix it, or talking about it, just move on.

So, you walk in the door after a long day of providing for your woman. She's frazzled, the house is unkempt, and the kids are running wild. You survey the damage and calculate a plan; before she can even begin to share her problems with you (because she will drone on and on about them), you offer up the solution now. Tada! Hero to the rescue! You should be rewarded because you can see it clear as day - you have the answer and this can be over. Let's fix this and fix it now so we can relax together.

But she has the strangest reaction to your fix. She's not happy that you've provided the solution. She wants to talk about it more, pile on even more problems; all the challenges, all the pain, all the detail. It's as if she wants to drag this out and make it as painful as possible. When she's in pain, you're in pain; so you cut her off again so she doesn't have to go through all that pain. She reacts even more strangely. She gets defensive and tries even harder to delve into the pain of the day. Now you're angry. You get louder trying to offer up your logical, succinct, and brilliant solution and she pulls the rug out from under you: she gets hurt by you. You see it happen, but it makes no sense to you, you can feel her pull away from you as she gets more upset and things have gone from bad to worse. You try to stay focused on the solution you've offered, but she keeps adding details that have nothing to do with the solution that you know will work. You get louder and more insistent, cutting her off over and over again so she doesn't get stuck in the pain that she seems determined to feel. She pulls further away from you, begins crying and suddenly you've lost the battle (even though you know you had the solution) and you have no clue how to fix this.

This repeats itself day after day, draining away the love. You begin to lose respect for her, you secretly wonder if she's crazy. Love has gotten hard and you see no relief in the near (or far) future.

Why Won't She Listen?

While men are the "fixers" of the universe, women are the "connectors" of the universe. Women have an innate drive (that they cannot turn off) to create connection and beauty everywhere they go. They are driven by these twin forces as strongly as you are driven to solve problems.   Women process this connection with others through their feelings, not through achievement or expediency. That's why she can't accept your fix. Her focus is on connection first, then fixing, and often connection IS the fix for women.

That's why she is constantly asking you how you feel - to create connection with you before she shares her solution. The more feelings she can share with you, the closer she connects with you.   Therefore the last thing she wants is her feelings to be denied or cut off in an attempt to create a solution, because that would cut off the connection she's trying to make with you. Connections come first. Solutions come second.

Don't make the mistake of thinking that she doesn't want a solution. Frankly she may already have her own solution perfectly well planned out! But what she wants is a connection with you. She is attempting to get that by sharing her feelings with you and asking you about your feelings. She has no idea that this strategy causes you pain and frustration instead of connection!

 When you cut her conversation off without listening to her feelings in an attempt to provide a quick solution, to her it feels like a physical cut. It hurts her, that is why she pulls away from you.   She may argue with you or defend herself, but eventually she will pull away from you (that is not what you want). Then she'll assume you think she's a ninny who can't fix things for herself. (Admit it, after a few rounds of this you do start thinking that.) You may even say things to her about being more logical and thinking her way through things, which disrespects her feelings even more. As you can imagine, if she is hurt and disrespected with each conversation with you, she will start to pull away from you more and more. At that point it becomes almost impossible for you to provide her with any solutions.

Warning!

Warning: when she stops sharing her feelings with you it is a very bad sign. It means that she is so hurt by you that she doesn't trust you with her heart anymore. This is when you'll notice that the light that shines out of her smile has dimmed around you. She'll turn to others to get the connection she so desperately needs - the connection she really wants from you.

There's a brilliant reason for her actions and it's not at all what you think. In order to be the connectors of the planet, women feel other people's emotions. As she goes about feeling these emotions all day long, the sensation is as if she is being filled with them. Towards the end of the day she needs to "empty" all she's collected during the day. Emptying happens through talking about it. Now, because she's been collecting emotions, as she shares them with you, it will be emotional: she feels other's pain, she hurts for others, she's happy for others, she's frustrated for others. In other words, she's connected to others. As she shares each emotion with you , she lets it go, all while making a stronger connection with you. Therefore the most loving, supportive thing you can do is let her share all of the emotions she's experienced during the day without shutting her down, cutting her off or trying to fix her.

Let's go back to you walking in the front door with everything out of control and she's upset. You believe she needs you to fix all that's out of control. That's not true. When a woman is upset, she will resist and reject instructions on how to do things better because she must process her feelings first before she can embrace solutions. She must get rid of the feelings. Then she can access her own solutions.

How Do I Win Her Back When She's Upset?

When a woman is upset, she needs you to simply listen to her while she talks about her feelings. You get extra points if you can empathize. You don't have to agree, you just have to acknowledge that she feels them. The worst thing you could do is to try to stop her from feeling them. To her that feels like they are being shoved back down her throat.

However, don't think you need to actually feel them. That's not necessary. You simply need to honor that she feels them. As she shares her feelings you can say, "Wow, that's tough, is there anything else?" or, "You've had a tough day." As she shares more, say or ask again, "I can see that hurts you." "I feel for you." "Is there anything else?" By allowing her to share all of her feelings, you do her the amazing service of allowing her to empty all she's carrying and connect with you. You become her hero simply by listening.

You can be the strong connection she needs when you stand by her side and simply listen to her while she's upset, weak, hurt, frustrated, sad or in pain. By allowing her to let it all go, she will come to the end of it quicker and develop a powerful need for you as the strength in her life.

Remember, don't stop her or make her wrong for having feelings and expressing them. Instead, give her twenty minutes of your focused attention simply listening to her. This shows her you love her in the way she needs to be loved. The process normally lasts no more than twenty minutes and then she'll be happy again.

Want more?

Go to:
http://www.livesuccessnow.com/more-win-influence/ for more free training.

Notes
1. Page 14: Who Switched Off My Brain? Audio Cd's, Dr. Caroline Leaf

Chapter Three for Men
Win Her Body:
Why Doesn't She Want Me Anymore?

"When we first got together we couldn't keep our hands off each other. It was hot, it was fun, it was often and I was happy. Now it's not. I'm lucky if she's interested once or twice a week...and some weeks go by with nothing. Why doesn't she want me anymore? It seems like I have to talk her into it and so often she's busy with something or someone else, like it's an imposition. What happened? I'm the same guy. It bothers me to have to ask. I don't understand what happened."

What happens to the passion, the fire, the burning desire we have for each other when we first fall in love? There's a daily (okay hourly) hunger for her burning in you and it doesn't go away. In fact, it's more like the more you get, the more you want. Why does it burn out for her so quickly? Said another way, what turns a woman off from her man?

I'm a big believer in marriage; and good sex is vital to keeping a marriage strong, long-lasting, healthy, and yes, fun! Many men believe that when they get married they now have a guarantee of regular and fun sex for the rest of their lives. That should be true, but all men eventually realize it's not. I've had a number of clients come to me because they don't have sex with their wives anymore, and they don't know what to do. I believe this is serious and it must be fixed.

The problem is not what you think it is. It is rare that she is directly rejecting you. Unless you have hurt her feelings in some way. Even if that is the case it's not so much about rejecting you as it is about healing her heart. Because a hurt woman has a very hard time opening up. While she is yours for life and you should have all the gratifying sex you could possibly want for the rest of your lives together, intimacy is never a given with a woman. It must be continually sustained by daily affection and caring conversation.

The problem is not even about her desire for you. You see, a man's sex drive is driven by the amount of testosterone flowing through every cell of his body. She doesn't have testosterone driving her every move all day long, making her ache for your touch.   In other words, she is not driven to want sex all day long by her body chemistry the way you are.

What Drives Her To Want You?

What drives a woman to want you is her emotions. While men are triggered by sight and touch, women are triggered by words and romance. It's the man whose words   touch her heart deeply that a woman will willingly and enthusiastically give her body to. Even then, it's still not a lifetime pass once you've touched her heart. I've already shared with you that a woman's heart must be continually won.   So even after you've won her heart, you must consistently make those emotional connections daily. The day that you don't touch her emotions is the day she won't be interested in giving you her body. Her heart is the key to touching her body.

All the things we've already gone over will work: talk to her, listen to her, let her be emotional, spend time with her. Now you can add to that: touch her in non-sexual but adoring ways, text or call her during the day when you are apart. All of these simple and easy things make her feel cherished by you and bind her heart to yours. In other words, if you do all the things you did to win her in the first place, you will continually win her, just don't EVER stop doing them.

Let me take this a bit further for you. I'll share with you the 3 most common reasons getting in the way of your intimacy, and of course what to do about them, so you can have the intimacy you both want and deserve.

She's Tired.

Women have bought the "Super Woman" myth. They believe they are supposed to work like a man, all day, then come home and be a woman who takes care of the children, cleans all night and still be there for her man. I recently heard an executive coach of some of the top female CEOs in the United States say he believes these successful women were actually killing themselves through their lifestyle. This could very well be true. In order to "do it all" a woman has to burn testosterone as her fuel much like a man does. However when a woman's body burns testosterone in high levels it also burns through her adrenaline stores.[1] The toxic combination of those two chemicals literally burn out her organs.

Many women are now experiencing adrenal burnout. A woman wasn't built to act like a man, nor is she fueled in the same way because she doesn't have the same equipment. That doesn't mean a woman can't run an organization or be a CEO, (ladies put down the pitchforks aimed at me please). It means that if she tries to do it in the same way a man does, it will cost her. Because of all of this women are tired! When a man is tired, he rests. When a woman is tired she keeps moving. Because she's tired, it makes it extremely hard to be passionate, open, involved, fun or even interested.

 The answer is easy. If she looks exhausted, she is and she needs rest. She needs a good night's sleep...let me clarify that: an uninterrupted good night's sleep. If you truly want to show love, try cleaning the bedroom, turning down the sheets, spraying them with a light, lovely scent, lighting some candles, putting on some soft music and taking her in there. Tuck her in, tell her how beautiful she is, tell her what your favorite body part of hers is (don't touch it or even look at it, just tell her about it), then tell her she needs to rest because tomorrow night (or morning if you can't wait) you fully plan on showing her how much you love her. Kiss her and **leave the room**. You'll be amazed at what rest does for a woman and her passion for you.

It's Too Loud.

I know this sounds strange, but what you don't know is women have a completely different experience when they walk into a room than men do. Because of her gift of a diffuse focused brain, when she walks into a room she doesn't so much see what's in the room, as she is assaulted by everything in the room.[2] The drapes beg to be opened, or closed, or straightened, or dusted, the table screams to be wiped down, the shoes wail to be picked up and put away, the dust on every surface calls out; anything out of order in the room screams for her attention. This makes it extremely hard to relax, ever. When it comes to intimacy it gets even louder: *Do I need to take a shower? Do I need to brush my teeth? When is the last time I shaved my legs?*

If a woman is already tired, adding intimacy to the load can be overwhelming. The fight to get her into the bedroom or even interested in sex isn't about you. It's about all the things on a woman's plate screaming at her to get done, which she can't turn off. If you can get her in the bedroom the screaming starts all over: the bed is not made, the clothes are lying on the floor, will the neighbors, or kids hear us? You don't realize what an amazing gift you have to be able to tune everything out and just get what you want. Women do not have this. So the greatest thing you can do for her is straighten the room before she gets into it. Close the drapes. Put on music so she doesn't have to think about sounds she might make that others can hear. This makes it safe for her and quiets the room so she can begin to focus on you. When she can finally focus on you and give herself into your passionate hands...everyone's life gets better.

She's Emotionally Far From You.

If you have touched a woman's heart, and made her feel emotionally close to you, she's much more interested in having you touching her body. That means if she's not responding to your touch, if she doesn't melt when you touch her, she is feeling emotionally far from you. If she flinches when you touch her that is a sign you have hurt her feelings. (go read Chapter four.) If she's not flinching, but she just appears not interested (not cold to you, but also not hot for you) she needs you to stir her emotions toward you. I'll give you some simple ways to do this.

Her emotions are the key to her heart and her body. You see, you use sex to connect with her emotionally, but she uses emotions to connect with you sexually. It can make a woman feel like a prostitute if you want sex before giving her an emotional connection with you. That means sex can actually make her feel bad instead of good if she hasn't been listened to, seen and adored before intimacy, rather than afterward (or even during).

Try this: think of all the things you love about her and begin sharing them with her. "I love your smile, it makes my heart jump when I see it...I love your touch, it's like the electricity that fuels me... I love how soft your skin is... I was in a boring meeting today and all I could think about was your skin... I've missed your voice all day... I love how hard you work and all the things you do around here..."

Like I tell my clients, sit down for ten minutes and make a list of all the things you love about her. Then keep that list handy, review it often, add to it regularly and use it daily. Warning: DO NOT READ HER THE LIST! That won't touch her heart and she will end up mad at you. Just talk to her every day about all the little things you love about her. Parcel it out, a few things from the list every day. You can write one of them on a steamy bathroom mirror one day. You can put a note in her purse another day. You can put a note in the refrigerator yet another day. A note in her car one morning.. Make it an adventure of love for both of you. After a few days of this, simply watch her while you are telling her all about the things you love about her, she will begin to respond and I know you know what to do once that happens.

Want to go deeper?

Go to:
http://www.livesuccessnow.com/more-win-influence/
for more free training.

Notes

1. Page 19: Understanding Women Audio Cd's Alison Armstrong
2. Page 20: Understanding Women Audio Cd's Alison Armstrong

Chapter Four for Men
Win Her Mind:
Why Can't She Get Over It?

"It's like the light has gone out of her. When I walk in the room, she leaves. I climb into bed and when I touch her she flinches and rolls as far away from me as possible. It's like there's an iceberg in the bed between us. At dinner she's uncommunicative, unresponsive and wants to leave as quickly as possible. If she stays in the same room with me she sits as far from me as possible. I know I've done something wrong, but I don't know what it is. When I ask her, she says, "nothing" in a dry, monotonous voice. I tried flowers but she just glared at me. I see that glare often. I don't have any idea what I did and I don't know what to do to fix it!"

My client was heartbroken when he finally called me. He'd lost the heart of his woman and he didn't have a clue how it happened, nor did he know what to do to get her back.

When you finally notice that your woman is upset with you, you immediately go into the "provide for her" mode. You may buy flowers, try to take her out, bring her chocolate or a cup of her favorite coffee, you may do yard work, or take out the trash. In other words you will work to provide something to make it better for her. As you do, you will also tell her all the things you are doing for her so you can get credit for all the points of the actions, hoping this will somehow solve her pain. But it won't work and it didn't work for my client either.

When a woman's feelings have been hurt by her man she takes it personally. When all you provide doesn't work, your next resort is to leave her alone to process it by herself. After all, that's the way you would deal with things. But she's not a man and she doesn't process the way you do. Since she has taken it personally, there is no way mowing the yard could solve her hurt. Leaving her alone to process it by herself will not allow her heart to resolve issues toward you.

Why Isn't Providing Enough?

What you have to realize is that a woman's emotions are a major part of her sense of self. Her feelings are what fuel her life. That's why her smile can light the world of anyone around her. Her squeal of joy can make anyone near her happy. She can be up one minute, down the next, riding a roller coaster of feelings from one moment to the next. Her emotions are what give her such explosive power to light up a room, or to light up your life. She is an emotional storm. Her capacity for feeling is much wider than a man's. Its a rainbow of emotions from light to dark.

However, when a woman's feelings have been hurt by you, her sense of self has been personally attacked. Leaving her alone or giving her time to "get over it" cannot heal that wound. When her feelings have been hurt, it's as though the light in her has been turned off. She experiences the world now as a dark, scary, lonely and painful place. There is no hope, there is no way out. She feels lost. The emotions of pain and fear crash onto her, imprisoning her in a dark place where it's hard to breathe, it's hard to think and it aches in every part of her being. Men have no understanding of this because they do not experience it.

How Can I Know I've Hurt Her Feelings?

You can know you have hurt your woman's feelings when you encounter any of these reactions: she won't look you in the eye, she won't talk to you, or she will avoid talking to you as much as possible. She doesn't want to be touched, she cries for no apparent reason, or she won't share her feelings with you. You get the "evil eye" and she pulls away from you, or she deliberately sits on the other end of the sofa or even leaves the room when you enter. She makes comments under her breath as if she can't be bothered to speak to you or they are snide comments designed to hurt you. Your typical reaction is: "This is ridiculous, buck up, just get over it and move on!"

Believe it or not, there are real reasons for her behavior. You see, when you get upset your body is flooded with a mixture of toxic chemicals; that's why you physically feel bad when you are upset: the headache, the muscle aches, the upset stomach, an inability to sleep.[1] Because you have a much higher level of testosterone than women do, that testosterone helps you burn through those toxic chemicals in about an hour. You also have the benefit of a single-focus brain. That means your brain thinks about one thing at a time, finishes it and then moves on to the next thing. Therefore, when you are upset you can simply put your focus on something else and within an hour your body has burned through the toxic chemicals while you are accomplishing something else.

When a woman is hurt emotionally, her body is also flooded with a mixture of toxic chemicals. It will take her body about twelve hours to burn through these toxic chemicals, because she doesn't have the benefit of the extra testosterone. That's twelve times as long to flush through all those chemicals. So when you think she's stewing over her hurt, you are right, but it's not because she wants to. It's because her body is flooded with chemicals that she can't burn through as quickly. In addition to that, there's another challenge. A woman doesn't have a single focus brain, a woman is gifted with diffuse focus.[2] That means she focuses on many things at once. Said another way: her brain can't focus on one thing at a time, it processes by connecting many things together.

What this means is that when a woman is hurt her focus often goes back to all the times she's been hurt before, magnifying the pain which will then release a new flood of chemicals that will take her body another twelve hours to process through.

Now she's flooded with emotional pain. This is why she can't seem to get over things once she's hurt. Her experience is as if she's imprisoned by pain. Her mind is overwhelmed by the present hurt and memories of previous unresolved hurts as well. She is stuck in a prison of darkness and pain until her body has processed through all the toxins, or she has resolved the problem. This is also why leaving her alone doesn't help. To her it feels the same as if you abandoned her when she's under attack. She wonders why you are so mean.

Hero To The Rescue!

The good news is that you have the key to help set her free and it's very simple. She needs a specific apology that will solve the problem and restore her feelings for you. This apology is so powerful, you don't even have to know what you did to hurt her feelings! (Sometimes trying to figure it out can cause even more damage). You simply need to acknowledge that her feelings are hurt and you had a part in it. Here are the six miraculous words that can set her free and get her over the pain quicker: "I'm sorry I hurt your feelings."

When you sincerely express these words to her, something amazing happens in her heart. Her feelings are acknowledged and her sense of self is supported and validated. When you acknowledge her feelings it's similar to the experience you have when she appreciates all of your hard work and you know how miraculous that can be.

WARNING!!! Don't Mess With The Recipe!

I am serious about this -- you must say specifically, "I'm sorry I hurt your feelings" and you must be sincere. You cannot say: "I'm sorry YOUR feelings are hurt" or "I'm sorry you got hurt". Also do not try, "I'm sorry you took it wrong and got hurt." Of course, never say, "I'm sorry your feelings get hurt so easily". Each of these versions will cause more damage because it is disrespectful to her feelings. Be her hero and give her the gift of : "I'm sorry **I** hurt your feelings".

You'll know it has worked when you see her take a deep breath and begin to relax around you. At that point, if she doesn't reach for you, ask her if you can hold her. DO NOT TOUCH HER WHEN SHE IS UPSET UNTIL SHE REACHES FOR YOU.   If she says yes, you are home free! If she is still holding back, try it again with: "I'm REALLY sorry I hurt your feelings".

What If It Get's Worse?

It's possible after you use the six miraculous words that it can appear to get worse. This is good news, not bad. You see, If there has been a lot of damage that hasn't been processed (healed in the past) she will begin to dump all the pain. This can sound like she is accusing you of all the things you've ever done to hurt her. Do not be disturbed, this is a good sign! It means she trusts you enough to begin dumping all the pain that has not been resolved. This way it will not be around to hurt her later. This means she is attempting to gain trust with you. I know this can be hard on you, but she needs you to not take this personally and stand firm while she's processing the old, unresolved pain. Just keep applying the healing balm: "I'm sorry I did that, I'm sorry I hurt your feelings," until she's done. Don't take any of it personally, it's like her heart is sick and she's dumping all the sickness in a safe place with you. When it has all been unloaded she will be the light of your world again and those old hurts won't be around to cause damage any more.

Want more?

Go to:

http://www.livesuccessnow.com/more-win-influence/ for more free training to take you even deeper.

Notes

1. Page 24: Deadly Emotions, Dr. Don Colbert

2. Page 24: Understanding Women, Audio Cd's Alison Armstrong

Chapter Five for Men
Win Her Attention:
How Can I Fix It For Her?

"She came home exhausted and upset and my radar kicked in. She'd had a hard day. She immediately began sharing how she got treated, how stressed out she was; even before I could catch my breath and focus on what she was saying. Before I heard her words, I heard the stress in her voice, someone was mistreating my woman. The protector in me rose up instantaneously: protect my woman, protect her now! I could easily see the answer before she could even finish her complaining. So I cut her off to get her out of the pain - now. This would solve it and solve it now, it was so simple, I could see it so clearly. But the strangest thing happened...she got more upset when I gave her the solution. It was like she wanted to hash this thing out piece by piece, but every piece seemed to hurt her more. I couldn't take it, I demanded she listen to me and stop doing what she was doing. That was a bad move. She didn't take it well at all, I got no "great idea honey, thank you for your help," nothing."

"It's so confusing talking to her because the more she talks the worse it gets. She's either upset about things that are none of her business, it's about what someone else is going through or she takes more on her plate than she needs to. She always takes on more than she should but she won't let me help. Help! It's painful to see my woman in pain but she won't let me help her."

Can you relate to this? You're not alone, it happens most every night to so many men when they come home to their women. The moment she opens her mouth with a complaint, any stress, whining or moaning of any kind, your "protector" rises up. It's magnificent the way you want to protect your woman, and it's painful when she won't allow you to. What can you do? Sit and watch her suffer and do nothing about it? Of course not, but since day after day goes on this way, you can't possibly be tortured anymore so you cut her off and try to fix it for her and if that doesn't work you remove yourself. You either leave the room so you can get some badly needed peace at the end of the day or you leave emotionally and intellectually: you tune her out and wait for the barrage to be over. When you do this, you know you have lost the battle to protect her, so you stop trying and you do whatever it is she asks you to do instead of what you know is right. When you abdicate you both lose.

I saw a video on Youtube that brilliantly models this called: It's Not About the Nail. It opens with a woman complaining about relentless pain, she can literally feel it in her head and she's scared it's never going to stop... the camera pans and you see she's talking to her man who can clearly see an actual nail sticking out of her forehead and he's concerned. He says, "Well, uh, you do have a nail in your head, I'll bet if we got that out..." She interrupts him and says, "It is not about the nail!" He can see the nail, but she doesn't want him to remove it and he tries to anyway. That makes her angry, she tells him exactly what she wants: "Stop trying to fix it. You always try to fix things when what I really need is for you to just listen." He replies, "See, I don't think that's what you need." They go round and round, and it's hysterical, I highly recommend you take the two minutes it takes to watch it (but not now, because the director, Jason Headley, doesn't give you an answer so keep reading and enjoy it after this chapter!)

Why Can't I Fix This?

Once again, it's not what you think. There's a great reason she's acting the way she's acting. You see, men and women use communication for two completely different reasons; you'll soon see it's actually opposite reasons. As a man you use communication to achieve, to get something done, to accomplish a goal, to provide something you want or need to provide for someone. You even have an unwritten rule that all men know: the fewer words you use the more points you get, the fewer words you use can actually demonstrate your expertise and your authority. Be concise, get to the point, always have a point and use communication to get it done or to prove your expertise. This is NOT how women speak, this is NOT why women communicate and that is why you keep running into the nail. In fact, there is no nail. The nail only shows up when you think you are talking to another man. You are not talking to another man, you are talking to a woman.

She keeps telling you it's not about the nail for her. That's because she uses communication for a completely different and opposite reason than you do. A woman uses communication to create connection, community and comfort. Since that is the goal, the more words she uses, the better. Its not about making a point because her diffuse brain connects everything to everything, so there can't be only one point. The more words she uses, the more connections she can make, and if those words cause her listener to feel what she's feeling it's a win-win! When the two of you are feeling the same thing- that is connection! She feels understood by you and cherished by you because you honor and share her feelings, instead of trying to stop her from feeling. Remember, feelings are one of her greatest gifts, it's what she was created to do and what brings the light to your life. When you take the time to feel what she's feeling without solving her emotions this allows her to be emotionally close to you. It's when she feels emotionally close to you she will want to be physically close to you as well. That means you will be having sex tonight!

Trying to stop her from feeling causes even more pain than she's currently in. I know you've experienced that, you just never understood why it worked that way or what to do about it. Her words, her conversation with you are intended to create a connection with you-preferably a feeling connection. When you think her conversation is an attempt to solve a problem, provide something, or achieve something and you move her in that direction instead of listening to her feelings, this shuts down her feelings, causing even more pain and distance between the two of you. That is the last thing she's after.

The 20 Minute Rule

So, let me make it easy on you. Your "presence" (focused attention on being with her, not doing for her) is the loving attention she needs every day. There is nothing else on this planet that affects a woman like the strength she gets when she can talk with her man. You cannot be replaced by talking to another woman. When she is seen, heard and has her feelings listened to by you, that is the most magnificent gift you can give her. When she can share all of her feelings and not be fixed, but rather adored for her ability to feel deeply this strengthens her like nothing else. It's an amazing gift you can give her. When she feels loved, cherished, seen, heard and felt by you...she gains the strength to go out and love others, create community, connection and make the world a better place with the gift that only femininity can bring.

Be the man she needs by simply listening to her for about twenty minutes. There is no other way. Her goal in the conversation is to share her day and to feel your presence. You get massive points if you allow yourself to feel what she's feeling so she can be close to you. After twenty minutes she will have sufficiently emptied the stress bucket of carrying all those feelings for others and have so much connection and passion for you, simply because you listened and were present for her. You will be her hero. Your presence is the greatest gift she can possibly have.

You don't have to remember the details of her story, just let her talk. She'll give you points if you remember places and times, but that's about all she wants from you. If you are confused by her rambling, you can ask her if she wants you to remember any details in particular and she'll tell you what's important to remember. If your protector gets riled up or if it starts to be too much for you, wait twenty minutes then ask her if she'd like to hear your solutions to what she shared. At that point she will likely be interested in your great ideas. That's when you can solve things if she actually needs anything resolved. Think of it as the twenty minute rule. No solutions for twenty minutes, simply listening is the fix.

What If She Won't Stop Talking?

If you'll listen to her for twenty minutes and stay focused on her, she won't go on and on and on the way she does now. It's likely she does that because currently your conversation does not provide her with the closeness and connection she so desperately wants. Finally, its fine to tell her after twenty minutes you can't focus any longer, ask if there is anything important she needs you to know and tell her you'd love to hear about the rest of it another time.

You are what she needs. Do not take your presence away from her. That is what kills relationships. She needs you to be there and listen to her every single day.

Want to go deeper?

Go to:
http://www.livesuccessnow.com/more-win-influence/ for even more free training.

Chapter Six for Men
Winning At Love: The Hero

I've shared with you in the last 5 chapters the 5 most common challenges I've found men experience.

Now, I'd like you to think about what it's like to be in relationship with you, from her point of view. You've learned what she really needs from you and how she needs to receive it. Rate yourself in the relationship from her point of view, what score would she give you?

RATE YOURSELF IN THE RELATIONSHIP
FROM HER POINT OF VIEW

1. How Can I Make Her Happy?

BEING PRESENT: How often are you present with her, focused on her and her needs in the relationship? Instead of abdicating the kingdom by coming home empty, tired, distracted, bored or boring?

1 = almost never	2 = sometimes	3 = half the time	4 = most of the time	5 = always

2. How Do I Handle Her When She's Upset?
LISTENING: Do you listen to her FEELINGS and try to be empathetic with them? Instead of interrupting her with a solution before she finishes a sentence?

1 = almost never	2 = sometimes	3 = half the time	4 = most of the time	5 = always

3. Why Doesn't She Want Me Anymore?

BEING CARING: How often do you notice if she needs rest, help with chores, or your attention? Instead of thinking more about what you want when you are with her, or grousing that she doesn't care about you?

1 = almost never	2 = sometimes	3 = half the time	4 = most of the time	5 = always

4. Why Can't She Get Over It?

BEING THOUGHTFUL: Do you respect her feelings regardless of what they are? Instead of cutting off her feelings or demanding she change them?

1 = almost never	2 = sometimes	3 = half the time	4 = most of the time	5 = always

5. How Can I Fix it For Her?
BEING THE HERO: How consistent are you at injecting love into the relationship in the ways she receives it? Instead of only giving what you want to give, when you think she deserves it?

1 =	2 =	3 =	4 = most	5 =
almost never	sometimes	half the time	of the time	always

Add up your score and total.
TOTAL SCORE _____

The Scoring Grades:

25 - 20 Points: YOU ARE HER HERO!

19- 15 Points: PRINCE

14 - 10 Points: LIGHT-WEIGHT

9 - 5 Points: MINION

4 - 1 Points: LOSING

How Would You Rate Yourself?

Take a solid look at yourself and grade yourself now. Would you want to be in relationship with you? Are you a HERO or are you LOSING at love? It's all up to you. You have all the power right now to transform your relationship. Your relationship can be saved simply by changing the way you show her love. You are hero of your relationship - unleash him.

It's typical to start out on fire with excitement for something, then with the passing of a little time the fire will begin to die down: we get distracted, or we simply focus on the next set of goals, we get bored, we get selfish or hurt or offended and as we do we will say things like: "She just doesn't make me happy anymore".

Since when was it her job to make you happy? If you are disappointed that she is not making you happy, I encourage you: this is just your wake up call to step up and begin to love at a higher level than you ever have before. Do it! Learn what it takes to really make your woman happy by loving her the way she receives love. Then everyday unleash that love on her. The rewards of living like this are magnificent: not only will she light up your life like nothing else in it, but you will become the biggest, best version of yourself and everyone in your world will be better because of how you show up in your own life. Our world is in desperate need of heroes, of you, you cannot be replaced.

Studies tell us happily married couples live longer, have higher and sustained levels of happiness, experience fewer diseases, have less chance of depression, make more money and raise healthier children to create a healthier society. It's a win, win, win. Truly, love is the greatest force on this planet and it's inside you now, waiting on you to step up, be the hero and unleash it on her and everyone in your influence.

Who Is The Most Powerful Person In The Relationship?

The most common complaint I run into is: "But, Genie, she's not interested in working on it!" She doesn't have to be. Never forget, the most powerful person in the relationship is you. What I've found in decades of doing this work is: if you will change, if you will inject love into a situation (any situation) the other person will change in reaction to your loving actions. You are the catalyst that changes everything. Sometimes it looks almost as if they don't have a choice because all humans need love: we can't live without it. When we don't get love in our current situations, we go looking elsewhere for it: but it is always our agenda - to find love. That's why affairs happen- because each of us is looking for love and if we don't have it in our current relationship, we go find it somewhere else.

That means love is always the answer- love is the ultimate answer. I've endeavored to show you how women receive love- I'm the first to say it is vastly different than how men receive love. In fact, it is the opposite of how men receive love. Love requires that you stop thinking about you, and start understanding her. Now doesn't that sound loving to you?

What Is The Greatest Thing You Can Provide For Her?

The greatest thing you can provide for a woman is a present, strong love that cannot be taken away or diminished by time or circumstances. This requires your focus to be on her, not on behalf of her. She wants you more than any "thing" you can provide. This is what every woman longs for, a man of her own who won't trade her in for a younger model. A love that deepens as the years roll by. A love that is legendary.

I'm going to tell you a secret that most men do not know. You know that sparkle you see in her? The one that makes your chest swell and your heart want to burst? That sparkle is her spirit reacting to the amazing gift of **your love**...that sparkle comes from you! It's the most extraordinary gift you can give a woman- a love that makes her shine with joy! Your love is what makes her so beautiful.

If you're missing love in your life, in your relationship, don't sit around waiting for someone else to make you feel good, to make you feel loved. That is abdicating the throne of your own life while you use others to make you feel better. It puts you in a losing position and it doesn't work. Don't spend all your attention and energy building your kingdom for her, only to find that she's left it to find love with another king who will be there with her, not a lonely palace he's provided for her.

Are You Up For The Challenge?

I dare you to be the captain of your own ship, to be the hero of your relationship and begin to inject love on a daily basis in the way she receives love (whether she deserves it or not, even whether you want to or not) and watch what happens in your life. Love is the greatest force on this planet and it's waiting on you to unleash it. When you do- you become more handsome, more courageous, stronger, more intelligent, healthier, more successful. It ripples through your life because love is a keystone habit, a habit that affects all aspects of your life. It's like a pebble being thrown into a pond, it flows over everything in your life. When you learn to unleash love in your relationships, the hero shows up and makes everyone's life better and the rewards to you are priceless.

The only way to lose at love is to stop giving it, because love never fails. What fails is giving her what you want to receive, instead of what she needs, because that isn't love.

Be the hero, provide the love.

Want more?

Go to:

http://www.livesuccessnow.com/more-win-influence/ for more free training.

Chapter Seven for Women
Influence Him:
Where Did My Romantic Man Go?

Ah, men. Maybe it's those rippling muscles bursting with strength, or his quick wit that makes you laugh, or his chiseled features focused solely on you, or his strength expelled on your behalf, or his daring feats designed to impress you, or the way he walks you down the street protecting you from traffic while his hand rests on your lower back steering you to safety...before you know it your heart is beating fast, you can't catch your breath, you flutter like a butterfly and don't know what to do with your hands. It's scary and wonderful all at the same time. A masculine man whose full attention is aimed at you feeds the heart of a feminine woman like nothing else. When a man adores you, it's as if he awakens a deeper, more beautiful version of you than you knew was in there and you become more beautiful than ever. He has awakened Sleeping Beauty. Truly the love of a man unveils the beauty of a woman like nothing else and it feels glorious.

You want to be loved. You adore the way men can make you feel. That's why Nicholas Sparks movies and Bella & Edward from The Twilight Series touch your heart so deeply. A man can make you feel as though you were the most beautiful, adored, cherished creature ever created. Its astounding what the love of a man can do to you and when you feel it, you will give up everything to be with him and follow him anywhere on the planet. (I know I did!)

Have you ever swooned when a man walked by and gave you that special smile just for you? I'll never forget when I was working with a young man who was doubting his virility. He was a highly accomplished man, he had won a silver medal in the Olympics. Yet because of some things that were said to him when he was in grade school, as well as a couple of painful, broken relationships (which we all have) he was struggling. After a few conversations he got re-centered, re-connected with his core and when he did, he flashed me a purely masculine smile and I swooned! It hit me like a wave knocking the breath from my chest. I took a deep breath, shook my head, got ahold of myself and cautioned him to use his powers for good at all times.

The Way Of A Man With A Woman....

Every woman knows the powers I'm talking about. When he sets out to woo you, it's as if his romantic soul knows no bounds. You are showered with attention and gifts. You've become the most compelling thing in his life and he wants to know everything about you and the conversations last many, many long delicious hours. His attention is solely for you, as he calls you again and again. hoping you'll spend some time with him. He's captivated by you and in the process he sets out to capture you, and does his best to win your heart. It feels wonderful to be pursued by a romantic man that makes your heart flutter. So, you give him your heart (or maybe he steals it with all the attention). He's The One and you are hooked.

Then, you know what happens...it cools off and the fairy tale is suddenly and rudely over. When you realize there is no happily ever after, you feel cheated. Typically it takes about two years for a passionate relationship to cool off, according to studies by Dr. Dorothy Tennov.[1]

Two years go by, then what happens? Truthfully, if you don't purposely do things to recreate the passion, the connection, the fun that came so easily, naturally and passionately; the vacuum that is left by that burning flame going out sounds like you're complaining which is met by his blaming, then your bickering which is met by his aggravated fighting, which is met with your hurt emotions that turn to cold bitterness which is met by his closed off stoicism and pulling even further away from you. These scenarios (which every love affair goes through, so don't despair) destroy your love from the inside out.

Why Is It Only About Sex Now?

This is when I will get a call from a woman wondering: "Where did my romantic man go? Now that he's got me, he's not even interested anymore. He leaves me to go to work, he leaves me to be with his friends, he leaves me to watch tv or surf the internet...Genie, he's left me! He won't talk to me all day and then he wants to have sex." You feel abandoned. You feel like it was a bait and switch scam that you fell for and now you've lost it all.

At this point most of you may begin to complain to him in an effort to get him to change back into the romantic man. You'll say: "Why don't you spend more time with me? Why don't you listen to me? Why don't you pick up your things? Why don't you help me? Why don't you care?" What does all of your complaining get you? Nothing. He pulls further and further away from you. Now he wants to spend less and less time with you. The weird part is you still love each other, you just can't seem to get along, to reconnect, to relight the fires of passion that brought you together. It is so painful for both partners and it doesn't have to be this way.

I do actually believe it is all part of a divine plan. I know how strange that sounds, but that's only because you don't understand the truth about real love. Real love is a devotion to the other person that doesn't depend on their reaction to it; real love is never moved by whether or not the one you love returns your love, nor it isn't dampened by a hard day or a lack of attention. It is a love that cares more about the other person than about self. It's only when the romantic chemicals have worn off and we now have to choose to act in love (at a time when we don't feel it, in fact we feel the opposite of it) that true love has a chance to blossom. I hope that sounds like good news to you, because if you are feeling like the love has left your relationship and the fires are out- it's the perfect time to step into real love and experience the real thing instead of a temporary chemically induced, counterfeit bonding that burns bright and quickly fades out.

When Influence Damages

At the start of the relationship he works hard to win you and then walks away to provide for you; and you work hard to get him and then spend the rest of your life trying to influence him to change... and no one feels loved even though you love each other. That's a broken system that causes immense pain.

Men don't realize why every woman must influence those she loves (as a matter of fact, they see it as nagging and meddling). The truth is that the heart of every woman wants to nurture, to create relationship, connection, community, it's a spectacular part of the gift of femininity. So a woman who starts out falling in love with her amazing man will eventually move into the next stage, which is to influence him. She wants to recreate that deep emotional connection that set the stage to fall in love in the first place. A woman wants to influence in order to bring back the love and connection.

If a woman feels as if there is a break in relationship with another woman she will complain to that woman. The other woman knows this is a call to come closer, it's not an indictment of a woman's character. Men have no idea that complaining is a call to come closer, even though all women know it. For in the world of men, a woman who complains about him is maligning his character. It's repellent and it has the opposite effect of what she desires: complaining pushes him away instead of bringing him closer.

In the next five chapters I'll share with you how you can influence your man in ways that he adores, in manners that truly nurture his hero heart, while calling the best of him to rise up and stoke the fires of passion between you again and again. Now, since you know complaining won't work with him: STOP IT. It poisons your love affair, it poisons the atmosphere. There are so many other ways to get what you want without destroying it.

So, Where Did My Romantic Man?

Let me start by telling you where your romantic man went: he went to work so he could take care of you. Once your hero has won your heart, he sets out to provide for you with all of his might: and I do mean all of his might. That's why when he comes homes he's empty, exhausted and has very little focus or energy for you. Providing for you is one of the most fulfilling things a man experiences and he takes it seriously. When a man says: "I'm doing this all for you," he means it.

Okay, okay, I can hear you complaining..."What about me, Genie? You mean I'm just supposed to put up with the empty shell that comes home; he doesn't want to talk, he doesn't pay me any attention and then when he finally does pay attention he wants sex! I'm supposed to just hop into bed with him when he has ignored me all night?"

Yes.

Don't get angry, let me explain. It's not what you think. He's not ignoring you (and I'll show you how to get his attention, how to get him to listen to you and how to get him to talk to you in the next few chapters). In the mean time this is what's really going on.

You see a man has a single-focused brain. What that means is he focuses on ONE thing at a time. One. That's it. There is nothing wrong with him. He was created to work this way, it is one of his greatest gifts. His brain will process through one thing at a time. When he's through processing that one thing, he can move on to the next item. When he comes home from work his brain is actually still at work. That's why when he comes home and you immediately start trying to talk with him to reconnect (even before he's gotten out of the car), he's either not there for you (you think he is ignoring you) or he's grumpy (which you decide is rejection, it's not). Most men need about 20 minutes to process through the end of work and mentally arrive home. Said another way, give his brain a chance to get home.

The 20 Minute Solution

The solution is very simple. Give him 20 minutes to get his brain home before you begin sharing your day or asking him **anything**. Give him 20 minutes of peace and silence. He really needs it so he can re-charge and be there for you and with you. It would be wonderful if you would greet him with a smile and a kiss and then walk away from him. I highly recommend you do this no matter what your day is like. Make this your own personal ritual- when you see your man, it automatically brings a smile to your face and he gets a kiss. This simple ritual will do wonders for both of you. This trains your brain that when you see your man, it triggers a smile & kiss. Thus wiring your brain for love for him every time you see him, instead of irritation every time you see him. Can you imagine the difference this will make in your relationship?

You'll know his brain has come home when he comes to find you. That's when he's finally present. Then you can share with him and he'll be able to focus on you.

CAUTION...

Warning: a man in an exhausted state cannot sustain long or multifaceted conversations, truly not even short ones. Seriously. He has that single focused brain to deal with and no energy. It makes it virtually impossible for him to focus on your 29 details in 29 seconds. It has **nothing** to do with whether or not he cares or is interested, or whether or not he loves you. When he's empty, he's got very little to give because he really has poured it out all day to provide for you. But don't despair because I know a secret...

Let's Talk About Sex...

There are two things that quickly re-fill a man's tank: sex with the woman he loves and appreciation. Here's what you don't realize: when your man feels emotionally far from you, sex is what he uses to feel close to you again. He doesn't need emotional intimacy the way you do, he needs to be as close to you as possible. That means when he reaches for you he wants YOU, not your body. Sex is how he shows you how much he's missed you and how very close he wants to be to you. He doesn't need conversation to get there, the way you do. He wants to be intimate with you. Words just prolong the separation in his mind. He is not a woman and he doesn't run on conversations that bring emotional intimacy. This is why I said, yes, you are supposed to have sex with him when he hasn't talked to you because you now know how badly he wants to reconnect with you each time he reaches for you. After he's reconnected with you in the most intimate way he'll have the capacity to carry on a conversation.

The Power of Appreciation

Secondly, after he's expended all he has to provide for you at work he expects (and deserves) to be met with appreciation, not complaining, not more problems that he doesn't have the energy to face right now, and not with an unhappy woman. Studies show that, once a base salary is met, men and women will work much harder for appreciation than for more dollars.[2] Appreciation is our reward for all of our hard work, especially for a man. Appreciation is a miraculous tool and it just so happens that sex is also his favorite form of appreciation.

I've watched my own husband come home from an extremely stressful day with nothing left to give; he's grumpy, he's complaining, he's exhausted and he's not nice to be around. When he hears me say, "Honey you went through that for me and the kids, to provide for us, you are such an amazing man, thank you." I can see his chest rise with pride and his strength return right before my eyes, and you will too. Appreciation is a great gift and it will recharge him almost as well as sex will. Appreciation is a wonder drug to any relationship.

Try it, be generous, appreciate him and all he does instead of complaining...it will bring him closer and relight the fires you both deserve.

Want more?

Go to:
http://www.livesuccessnow.com/more-win-influence/
for more free training, audios & videos.

Notes

1. Page 37: The 5 Love Languages, Gary Chapman

2. Page 40: <u>Glassdoor</u> revealed that more than 80 percent of employees say they're motivated to work harder when their boss shows appreciation for their work, compared to less than 40 percent who are inspired to work harder when their boss is demanding or because they fear losing their job. Chad Brooks Published: 11/19/2013 05:08 AM EST on BusinessNewsDaily

Chapter Eight for Women:
Influence His Soul: Why is He So Bossy?

"I had a tough day and I knew it was gonna get worse the minute he got home. Dinner wasn't ready, the kids had me outnumbered and were in complete rebellion and I looked and felt like I had been through hell. I don't understand why he can't just give me a little sympathy, some caring, that's all I need. No, he's gotta walk in the door and start barking orders at me like I'm an incompetent fool who can't handle life. He's mean as he tells me how I need to fix this and do that, and each sentence gets louder if I respond. He puts me down and makes me feel like an idiot, as if I don't know how to do anything. My bad day gets worse the minute he walks in. I used to look forward to him coming home. Now I cringe."

This was a client of mine. Her dictatorial husband was making her life so much harder on her with every one of his attempts to help her. She felt like she had to defend herself instead of feeling supported, cared for, or helped by him. When she had to defend herself, she was not interested in talking to him, and was certainly not interested in sex with him. Not to mention it's a very bad sign for your relationship if you cringe at the thought of him coming home.

The good news is that being bossy was not his goal nor his intent and it's not your man's either.

Bossy. What Is It Really?

What she didn't realize is that men are born problem solvers.   One of their favorite words is "problem." Women don't like the word problem.   We like "challenge," "opportunity," "complication;" anything but "problem." Men love the word "problem" because their favorite thing to do is provide a solution, to be a hero. They were made to do this. In fact, men's brains are wired to provide quick solutions. They have fast decision making wiring in their brains and they love to use it.   While emotion will trigger irrational thought in a woman, emotion actually triggers solution mode in him; you know this as Mr. Fix It. Your emotions will trigger him to look for solutions. Mr. Fix It is one of his favorite modes because it means he can provide something for you that makes a real difference in your life, and wow, making a real difference in your life is something he lives for.

Sounds great, doesn't it?   But it rarely feels that way because between his overeagerness to provide something he thinks you need or what he believes will be helpful, as well as his automatic problem solving brain, he runs you over while trying to fix things for you. That's exactly what my clients' husband was doing unknowingly. He was trying to help but he made it so much worse by the way he delivered the "help."

There were a few things my client needed to know to make her life so much better.   First a man prefers to process troubles and thoughts when he is alone.   He won't talk it through like you do, he prefers to think it through alone, without interruption. This is normal, healthy male thinking. It's only after he has determined his answer that he will start talking about it and share it with you. Then when he shares he will typically share the answer first, not the deliberations to get to the answer as you do. This is because his brain has a 38% larger temporal lobe than yours- he uses this part of his brain to sort things out by himself.[1] What that means is, if you are talking about troubles without offering a solution immediately, to a man's brain that means you must not have a solution. Therefore talking about troubles without declaring a solution first is the same as waving a red flag in his face for him to fix it for you. It's not that he thinks you are stupid, in his mind the best thing he can do for the woman he loves is come to the rescue and give you a solution; the quicker the better. He never wants to see you suffering, and it doesn't occur to him that running over your feelings to get you to the solution is hurtful. His tunnel vision doesn't see feelings. It sees solutions.

Why He Cuts You Off And Doesn't Listen

In his haste, he'll cut you off before you even finish a sentence, but it's not because he doesn't care about your feelings. In fact, its exactly because he cares about your feelings and wants you to feel better immediately that he cuts you off. Mr. Fix It means to serve you, to love you, to provide for you! Mr. Fix It never means to harm you or run over your feelings or make you feel badly (its such a shame at how often this happens though).

Secondly, because of the size and shape of the part of his brain called the corpus callosum (this is the part of the brain that connects the right and left sides together) his brain separates emotions from thought. This keeps him level headed, even toned (yes, you might say cold at times).   This is so important because he thinks if you are emotional there is something really wrong in your life and then his Hero mode kicks into gear.

Are you getting this?   Now we've got Mr. Fix It and Hero stepping in together, running you over, hurting your feelings, being dictatorial to fix it for you - NOW. All of this is fueled by his desire to bring you much good in life, to provide the best he can for you! That's why he comes across so bossy!

Why He Get's Loud

But that's not all!   I've already shared with you that when a man's tank is on empty he has a very hard time providing anything. That doesn't mean he won't try. It means that as he tries, it will come across as loud, rude, domineering or even oppressive. It's not because he thinks you are a ninny who can't figure it out for yourself, it's because tired people are grumpy. It should be great news to you that all of the things that hurt you are actually meant to help you.

What I did for my client was train her how to handle Mr. Fix It and Hero turning into Dictator every night. Once you realize that his behavior is meant for good; it's actually his big heart trying to make things better for you, there are just a few simple, two degree shifts in how you handle Mr. Fix It, Hero and even Dictator that transform everything so you can love and be loved again. Because a man has an unconscious drive to provide, and it's something he can't turn off, working with this drive instead of against it makes all the difference.

The secret is understanding that he is actually trying to provide something for you. Now lets look at how you can do that.

How To Influence Him From Bossy to Helpful

So let's go back to her hard day and he's about to walk in the door. The kids are still in insurrection, the house is still a mess and dinner is not ready. She's worked hard all day long too, and she's got another three or four hours of work staring her in the face before she can end her day. In walks our exhausted Hero. Before she notices him he is regaled by a round of "Daddy, Daddy, Daddy," jumping, screaming, yelling, demand and requests for attention and every other thing kids can think of. Our exhausted hero eventually comes looking for the love of his life and finds her upset, exhausted and wanting some help. He has left his battlefield at work only to walk into another one at home and his brain is not home yet (it will still take him 20 minutes to be fully there).

I had her use the ritual she'd begun to implement: when she saw him it triggered a smile on her face and a kiss on his mouth. I had her say, "Ah, my hero's home!" and smile when she did it, so she would immediately feel better just by seeing him. Then she gave him his 20 minutes alone to process coming home. When he came in to check on her because his brain was finally home then she greeted Mr. Fix It with, "I'm so glad to see you, I have a problem and I need you." Now that his mind is home, not just his body, he can focus on being the provider he loves being. He's been appreciated, honored and he's focused and ready to help (instead of helping in an angry, exhausted, just get it done state that makes her feel as if he's running her over).

He's a very different man at this point than the Dictator. Then very succinctly, she was to tell him ONE thing to do to help her out. If she just wanted him to listen to her and show he cared, she would tell him, "I just need you to listen to me while I dump this rotten day's details. It would make me feel so much better if I could just talk about my day for ten minutes. All I need from you is to listen. You don't have to remember anything and I don't need you to fix anything. I just need to talk it out of me and then I will be happy to be with you." This way he knew exactly what she needed and could easily provide it without Mr. Fix It running her over.

If she needed help with the dinner or the kids then she would ask him for ONE thing and be very clear about what it was that she wanted, always adding how happy it would make her if he would provide it. Remember, the provider drive in him never turns off, so he's happy to provide if he knows exactly what will make her happy. This makes it a win for both of you, he knows what to do and she gets what she needs, not what he thinks she needs. This is important because if she doesn't let him know what will make her happy, he will provide what he thinks will make her happy. Unfortunately, he doesn't think like she does, so what he gives often isn't what she wants, even though it's coming from a heart of love. That's when things get ugly.

What About When He Wants to Provide Something I Don't Want?

If he does try to provide you with something you don't want, you can reply with:

"Thats a good idea, thank you, but that's not what I want right now." or even "Thanks, that's not how I've decided to handle it." If you do it this way he's been honored (listened to) and appreciated so he'll be much more agreeable. In addition since you are giving him an indication that you have an answer he won't feel so compelled to run over you to get you one.

Want to go deeper?

Go to:
http://www.livesuccessnow.com/more-win-influence/ for more free training, audios & videos.

Notes
1. Page 43: Who Switched Off My Brain? Audio Cd's Dr. Caroline Leaf

Chapter Nine for Women
Influence His Body:
Why Won't He Listen to Me?

"When we first met he was amazing. We would talk for hours and hours about anything, everything, nothing. I adored talking to him and he wanted to know everything I thought. Now he won't listen to anything I say and most conversations end up in arguments and I'm not even sure why. I was talking to him about something and before I knew it we were in an argument yelling at each other! I was just sharing and suddenly he's attacking me! It doesn't make any sense and I have no idea why that happens. Then he says I'm illogical, I don't make any sense, I don't have a point. He just makes me feel so stupid no matter what we talk about. Talking to him is frustrating and painful. I'm so lonely. Did I marry the wrong guy? I don't know if I can take this any more."

The Big, Ticking Time Bomb!

All right, we've hit the mother-load...this is the big, ticking, time bomb in relationships (especially for you): communication. It seems everyone knows the importance of communication, because without it there is no relationship. However just because you are talking to each other doesn't mean he has a clue what you are saying or visa versa. The problem actually isn't that he's not listening to you; the fact that you argue demonstrates that he is listening to you, it's just that what you say means something else to him.

Even though it sounds the same, the experience is we are actually speaking two different languages. Seriously. I heard Alison Armstrong call what men speak: Menglish. That really resonated with me. I began calling what women speak Feminish in order to help distinguish the differences in communication. Though they both sound like English (or whatever language you speak), they are two different languages spoken for two different reasons, designed to get two different outcomes. You see men speak and listen only to determine actions and solutions, while women speak and listen for feelings and connections. You'll soon see we talk in opposite directions and this is where all the problems are born.

Men use communication for a very specific purpose: to accomplish something, to make a point, to solve a problem, to get something done, or to provide something. That's it. (Notice those are all the same thing)

Understanding "Menglish"

Men love bullet points, fast, get to the point conversations that always have a logical point (get the point?). In fact they have an unwritten rule that states "the less you speak the more you demonstrate your expertise." Get that, the fewer words the better in Menglish. Men say what they mean and mean what they say and do it as concisely as possible. They hate to repeat themselves. Often in the midst of a conversation they won't even respond when you talk to them, they'll just give you a grunt or a head toss because the fewer words he uses the better, and if you didn't have a point he has nothing to respond to.

This is why when you ask him how his day was he says. "Fine." That's it, nothing else. You have to dig for more if you want more. That does not mean he doesn't trust you, he's not interested in you, or he's angry at you (the way it would if you were talking to a woman). It just means he's speaking "Menglish" and that is a complete and full answer.

This is not how you speak or use communication. You use communication to make emotional connections with others, as many connections as possible. The more words the better, the longer the conversations the better and having a specific point is optional at all times. You want people to feel good by talking with you. You desire to make connections with others by saying what you think they need to hear instead of what you actually think.

Your concern is for their feelings over giving them your personal opinion. You use conversation to nurture others, wanting to make sure you've heard all they need to share. You also leave lots of leeway in your conversation for interpretation so others are not offended by any of your opinions. This is the real point of conversation for you: to make a connection. In addition, you also use conversation as a way of deciding on a course of action; it is thinking out loud. Men think out their actions in silence long before they ever share them.

This is why the longer you talk, the less he is able to listen. He'll get louder and shorter and try to pin you down for a point. So you keep talking. HIs frustration rises with each sentence you add. He'll begin to pick fights. "Why are you telling me this? I don't understand!" My husband actually said to me (very loudly): "I can't understand you because you just keep talking!"

Men start conversations with their answers. In Menglish, it is more efficient to start with the answer and it proves how capable he is. You start conversations with questions, to create interaction and connection. You want to know everyone's opinion, thoughts and feedback.

Men use conversation to complete tasks, to get things done. That means he needs to get moving and stop talking to go get it done. You use conversation to create relationship. Relationship is formed by long conversations. Men love the word "problem"- it's like a go sign to prove their masculinity and expertise. You hate the word "problem" and avoid it.

Men keep their emotions to themselves especially in conversation, they don't ever want to appear or feel weak. You share your emotions with others using lots of conversation, you want to feel empathy with and for others no matter what you or they are feeling. Men think and process in silence. You think and process out loud.

Men want conversations that are linear, logical and come to a conclusion quickly. Extra words are inefficient and a waste of time and energy to men. You want conversations that create a consensus with all involved, everyone should have a say and be listened to. You use words to create connection, content, and express your feelings. The more feelings (and words) the more connections you make, the better your relationships..

Men talk in facts, figures, logic and solutions. You talk to inform others of your feelings, their feelings, and his feelings. This creates understanding and eliminates stress while giving and receiving support. Men minimize problems in conversation to reduce stress. You make problems bigger to create as many connections as possible, because it's in connection with others that you minimize stress. Men stop talking to relieve stress, talking makes them feel worse. Also, when you keep talking it makes them feel worse. You talk to relieve stress, because talking makes you feel better. The more you talk, the better you feel. Men talk about one thing at a time. You talk as if everything is connected to everything, because of your diffuse focused brain, it all is connected.

Looking at the differences between "Menglish" & "Feminish," now you can clearly see why it can be so hard to talk to him, but it doesn't have to be. A few simple tweaks and you can hold his loving attention again while you talk.

He's Listening For One Thing

First, it's important to realize he IS listening to you, he's listening for ONE point that he can fix for you. When he doesn't hear it he gets lost, frustrated and angry in the process. That's why it quickly goes to loud arguments and fighting. He's actually fighting to fix things for you, he just doesn't know what it is you need.

Secondly, give him a point. Tell him exactly what you need from him so he can focus during your conversation and follow along much easier. Because of his single focused brain too many points can be painful for him. That's why he gets angry the longer you talk and the more points you add to the conversation. You can say, "Honey I just want to share my day with you, there is no point other than to see your handsome face while I talk. I need you to listen for 20 minutes while I ramble." This lets him know the point and the time frame and what he can provide, so he can relax and enjoy you.

Don't Do This

Thirdly, if your conversation is filled with complaining at him (letting him know that he is your problem) you will lose him. I've already suggested you stop complaining, let me reiterate: stop complaining at him as if he is the problem. It does great damage because in his mind, if he is the problem he must leave you to make it better for you.

There is a good reason for this: it's not because he's egotistical or selfish or refuses to change. This is also a reflection of his body chemistry. You see, because of the amount of testosterone running through him, he builds his self-esteem through maintaining independence. He correlates independence with strength. When you consistently tell him he's wrong, it's actually received as an attack on his strength as a man. Said another way: he takes your complaints against him very personally, as if he wasn't a good enough man for you. Because of his drive for independence he would be weak if he changed for anyone who complained at him. In addition, when he gets too close to you emotionally (which is what you are after) he actually experiences a drop in testosterone that makes him feel weak.[1] When that happens he has to physically leave you to regain his normal levels of testosterone so he can continue to provide for you and protect you. Don't be concerned, it just means he needs some time apart from you to regain his strength. Then he'll come running back. This is why freedom is so important to men, it takes freedom to keep him strong and healthy.

REWARD!

Finally, reward him for listening to you with great amounts of appreciation. " Thank you for listening," "That's a great idea," "You make me feel so much better," "My life is so much better just because you listened," "I'm happy now. You make me happy because you listened to me." I appreciate how you helped me by listening." This is so important. If he gets rewarded instead of complained at he will want to provide a loving, listening ear more and more.

Want to go deeper?

Go to:
http://www.livesuccessnow.com/more-win-influence/ for more training, audios & videos.

Notes
1. Page 50: Dr. John Gray audio

Chapter Ten for Women
Influence His Mind: What About Me?

"He runs me over, like my opinion doesn't count. He either makes decisions without me and just announces what he's decided we are going to do, or he cuts me off when I'm trying to decide something with him and informs me what to do. He won't even listen to what I have to say about it and it really hurts my feelings. The more I try to talk about it, the angrier he gets.   It doesn't matter if it's something for me or something for us. For instance, our anniversary was coming. I mentioned a great 5 star resort at the beach. Once he heard that he suddenly had blinders on and that is where we were going, period. As I researched it and discovered how ridiculously expensive it was I changed my mind, I wanted to do something else. His insistent reply was, "That's what you want, you should get what you want, just make the reservations."

He had made the decision right then, I had my orders and that was the end of it.   He does this to me all the time, I know that if I try to say anything, we will end up in an argument; I have been in this battle before. He was going to give it to me whether I still wanted it or not. It's not that it wasn't a wonderful trip, its the feeling that it's being shoved down my throat.

So often he just makes decisions and tells me what we are doing, without considering me, my thoughts or feelings, without talking to me or even allowing me to talk it through. Then if I'm not super appreciative he's angry because he worked so hard to give it to me! What about me? How do I get a say in things, how do I get what I really want?"

Ah, my client had been run over by "The Great Provider." I've talked to you in previous chapters about his driving desire to PROVIDE for you. I've mentioned this is an unconscious drive he can't turn off. Because of that it can often feel like you've been run over. He'll decide unilaterally how to move forward and you are not consulted. It feels more like you are commanded and shut down. It doesn't matter whether the provision is for you, for him or for the both of you--"The Great Provider" has spoken and that's the end of it. The more you try to discuss it with him the louder and angrier he gets, as though you have no say-so in the matter whatsoever.

Sometimes its like getting a present you don't want but he's determined to give it to you because he's decided that is what you should have.   For instance, one birthday my man brought me a bottle of wine when he came home from work. He was so pleased with himself that he remembered my birthday and had stopped to bring me a bottle of wine. As he handed it to me with a big kiss and said, "Happy birthday!" He was supremely pleased with himself; you could see it all over him. I kissed him and said, "Thank you, you are so good to me."   He opened the bottle, poured me a glass and waited for me to take a sip. I took a sip and once again said, " Mmm, thank you." Then I put the glass down and went to do something in the other room. When I came back he reminded me that he bought me wine for my birthday. I said, "Yes, you did, thank you my love."

Doesn't this sound like a wonderful evening? Here's the problem: I really don't like alcohol. I drink very little and would be happy to never drink at all. He likes alcohol, really likes it. He was giving me something he liked and apparently had completely forgotten that I don't like alcohol. For the rest of the evening he kept bringing it up, he kept saying, "I bought you wine I thought you would like, why aren't you drinking it?" He wanted to be rewarded for his effort. I didn't want to reward him for something I didn't want. In fact, I was a bit peeved he didn't remember I don't like alcohol. It felt like he kept putting pressure on me to drink something I didn't want, and to be happy about it and reward him for what he had done. "The Great Provider" struck again. This is a simple example that happens almost daily in relationships.

The real problem is that The Great Provider can show up as The Dictator. His decisions are decreed as laws that cannot be questioned or discussed. Many times the decisions are not vital- like a bottle of wine I didn't really want, but there are those times when it's an important decision and you need to have a say in things. It's necessary for you to be heard. The good news is there is a way to have him listen to you in the big decisions and the small. I'll walk you through how to stop getting run over by The Great Provider and get your needs met.

When The Great Provider runs over you it can often feel as though he's The Great Selfish, Egotistical, Unfeeling Jerk. It's all about him, he makes the decisions and what you want doesn't matter. Your job is to put up with his choices, no matter what they are and be happy about it. This can be painful. The good news is this is pretty far from what's really going on. With some understanding of what's driving him you'll know how to get your needs met.

There are three things going on in him that I want you to be aware of.

The first thing I want you to see is the responsibility of providing for you that he carries. Remember, this is not something he can turn off, it is an unconscious drive in him. It's similar to your drive to create relationship, it's not something you can turn off.

The Great Provider is committed to providing for his Beauty. This is one of the largest sources of fulfillment and satisfaction in his life. He is driven by his responsibility to provide and it weighs heavily on his mind at all times. What you don't realize is this isn't only about providing finances, although that is a huge part of it. It's everything he does for you as well. He will work all week and work around the house all weekend. It's all his responsibility and it weighs very heavily on him. He pours himself out to provide for the one he loves and everything he does for you is a form of provision. This includes taking out the trash, taking you to dinner, keeping you safe, fixing the car, building a fire for you....EVERYTHING he does for you is him providing for you. This is why he will present you with a litany of tasks he's performed for you expecting you to give him points and reward him for each individual act. "Honey I washed the car, I mowed the lawn, I took out the trash"...he'll itemize his good deeds like Sir Galahad had just saved the world, looking to you for his rewards. You of course, have done triple the amount of work and look at him like: so?

This is destructive because it's not about who does more work. It's about acknowledging what he has provided and the amazing reward only you can give him for being "The Great Provider." You are his greatest reward, you are why he does what he does and nothing can replace your appreciation. Your appreciation and honor (which is love to him) are why he does what he does. This is so important to him that he is constantly evaluating if he is a good enough provider for you, his Beauty.

When he is at work it is about providing for you, if he brings home a paycheck regularly and doesn't get appreciation it can dampen his efforts. When this happens you will hear him say he feels used, like he's nothing more than a paycheck. If he's driving you to dinner he will focus on getting you there safely (so single focused that he won't even hear you talking to him during the drive). If anything happens along the way, traffic is bad, or an accident happens, he takes it as his responsibility not the other driver's; he couldn't keep you safe. When you get to the restaurant if he can't find a good parking space he judges himself. If the waiter takes too long to serve you he's the one who's done a poor job of providing for you (not the waiter). If you send your dinner back he judges himself (not the chef) as if he didn't provide a good dinner for you. If you are not having fun he thinks he did a poor job of providing for you.

It never occurs to him that he is not responsible for your emotions. Sometimes you want to be quiet, or peaceful, or resting, or even melancholy, it's not always about being happy for you. There is nothing wrong with other emotions and connecting with others in what might be considered negative emotions can be a positive experience for you.

Even when it comes to sex, if you don't have an orgasm, he judges himself as not having provided well enough for you. You may have totally enjoyed the encounter with him. He is unaware it doesn't take an orgasm for you to be satisfied so he judges himself. I can't stress to you enough how much this drive to provide is underlying all of his actions and thoughts.

That's just the beginning of what's going on in him that you can't see. Because in addition to the commitment of providing for you, now you can see the the weight of the responsibility he also carries. He will pour all his energy out at work during the day and come home empty because of his commitment to provide for you. His single focused brain keeps him focused on work and nothing but work while he's there, until he's empty, then he comes home. However, if you need him at home and he's on empty he will show up for you there as well. When he's on empty the weight of it is much heavier than it needs to be so it comes out sounding like a grouch; grumbling and complaining. Yet he will still provide unless he truly has nothing left to give.   The grumbling, complaining and grouching is an indicator of his energy level and ability to focus on what you need. The weight of the responsibility shows up for him in how much energy he can commit to giving you based on how much he's committed to other responsibilities in his life. This is important because it's affecting every decision and most women are unaware of it. Because most women don't monitor their energy, they just keep going even when they are exhausted.

Finally, the last piece of this puzzle I want to reveal to you is that he believes he is the leader of your family. It's his responsibility to lead and to protect you. This is why he tends to think things through on his own and then present you with the direction he's decided he can lead you in. As he thinks his way through each decision he will weigh these four things: his responsibility up against his energy, his ability to lead in the decision and his ability to keep you safe.

If he thinks the decision will affect your future more than it's worth, he will say no. If he thinks he won't have the energy to provide what you are asking for, he will say no. If he thinks the cost is a good investment for the future, he will demand it. If he thinks you won't follow his leadership, he will say no. If he thinks you will be unsafe in any way, he will say no. These are not negotiable in his mind because everything thing in him is wired to provide for you and protect you, so they can come across as The Great Selfish, Egotistical, Unfeeling Jerk. He doesn't mean it that way at all. In his mind he's just trying to do his job.

I hope by now that you can see how good all of this actually is. Now let me show you how to work with it instead of against it, so he can be The Great Provider and Leader and you can be heard and an integral part of the decisions instead of the recipient of them (whether you like it or not!).

Mistakes To Avoid

When he gets loud and angry, he is experiencing pain of some kind. He experiences pain in conversations with you in three typical ways: danger, lack of appreciation and disrespect.

1. If he believes you will be in danger he will answer "no" every time.

2. Because of how important providing is to him, when he provides something and doesn't receive an appropriate level of appreciation, it can be very draining for him. If he feels he has poured himself out in providing and is not appropriately appreciated he will become grumpy, bitter and angry and his natural generosity to provide for you will begin to dry up. Even then, he won't stop

providing. He'll just become much more selective about what he's willing to provide. Often this can appear as The Dictator decreeing what will and will not be provided.

3. Responding to all of his decisions with questions can threaten him and trigger arguments. While you want to talk through everything, talking in itself is a reward for you. He doesn't want to talk. Talking is more draining than rewarding. In addition, when you question his decisions, he often takes it as if you don't think he knows what he's doing. This can be received as a lack of love on your part. That's because respect IS love to a man, and questioning all decisions is disrespectful.

If you are constantly correcting all his decisions you are on dangerous ground. No leader will put up with that, including your man. If you keep it up, no conversations will happen. Finally, don't try to talk through every decision with him. He can take that as an affront to his leadership. Once again it is received by most men as disrespectful and unloving.

Do This Instead

In the next thirty days I challenge you to begin to appreciate everything he does. Keep a running journal of all the things he's doing so you can become truly aware of what he does provide. Then daily thank him and appreciate him for each thing. You will be stunned at how much more he will show up for you because the reward of your appreciation is priceless to him (it's all he's ever really wanted).

Respond to his decisions with appreciation first: "Good idea, honey." "Wow, you want to provide us with that? That's very generous of you." "You take such good care of us." Then he won't feel disrespected. You can then add: "That's not gonna work for me," or "I don't really want that." "Would you like to hear why?"

Once he's been honored and appreciated he will be thrilled to know what it is you do want provided. Then be very clear on what you do want so he can easily see if he can provide it. Always add, this will make me happy or I'll be happy about it so he can see the appreciation and reward ahead of time.

Honor his sense of responsibility- When he gets loud, angry, even belligerent you can simply ask him: "Have I disrespected you in some way?" Or say, I meant no disrespect. He'll let you know what you said that caused the anger and it will soothe the wounded beast in him so you can talk through things again. Remember though, he doesn't want to talk things through at the level you do: he want's bullet points, so let things go easily and quickly.

If you want to discuss something instead of immediately questioning him say: "I know you have reasons for that, I'm curious, what are they? This honors his leadership instead of thwarting it. He'll be happy to share his reasons and talk things through with you because now his decision isn't under attack.

If you do disagree with his decision, simply say: "That's a great idea honey, but that's not gonna work for me." "I want this, at 5:00, and I will be happy."

Be direct about what makes you happy and tell him clearly so he can provide it. I'd like to go to dinner Friday night at 6:00 at my favorite restaurant: Joe's. This will make me so happy.

Want to go deeper?

Go to:
http://www.livesuccessnow.com/more-win-influence/ for more free training, audios & videos.

Chapter Eleven for Women
Influence His Attention:
Why Doesn't He Have Time for Me?

"I love my husband, but I don't like him and he really drives me nuts. He works all day then he comes home and he has no time for me. He'll veg out in front of the TV until dinner is ready. At dinner he doesn't want to talk, he doesn't want to help with anything unless he's directly asked. Like he can't see I need help without being asked. He acts like a zombie, non-responsive all night, then he wants sex before he passes out. When the weekend comes and I think he is actually going to have time for me, he wants to spend time with his buddies, fishing, golfing, basketball or he'll spend all day watching the game. Even that's not enough. Then he's got to watch the shows that talk about the game he just watched! He's got no time for me and then he says he loves me. Do you think he still does love me or did he just marry me for sex? I wonder."

The thrill is gone. The relationship is all work now and very lonely for both of you. This is a dangerous time in a relationship. What do you do when your love affair burns out and what's left is work and you don't even like each other anymore? I do believe this is a stage of relationships we all go through, but what you do about it can make or break you.

MIAH

My client ran into a MIAH: a missing in action husband. This can be terribly confusing, lonely and very painful. It's especially upsetting because you can see the problem is not that he doesn't have time: he's watching the game, he's golfing, fishing, playing....it's that it appears he doesn't have time for you. The pain comes from thinking he doesn't want you for anything but sex.

While you work hard to be there for him because you love him and want to spend time with him: you work all day, you make the meals, do the shopping, clean the house, fit in a workout to keep in shape for him, you diet, you run his errands for him. Every night you try to talk to him so you can be a part of his life.

When it gets too lonely you ask him to go to the movies with you, you ask him about his feelings to try to figure out what the problem is. You ask for a date night and you resent that you have to ask for it. What are you met with? A zombie who doesn't want anything from you but sex: a MIAH.

Don't get me wrong, he should have time with his buddies to just be a guy and act like a guy, it's equally as important as it is for you to spend time with your friends and just be a girl. Time apart is very healthy for the relationship. It allows you to reconnect with your femininity and allows him to reconnect with his masculinity, to miss each other and to come back together wanting that special spark that the other one brings that cannot be found with friends. Missing each other is a great gift to give your relationship but when you are missing each other when you are together, that needs to be resolved.

There are times he will sit and watch tv with you but that means he's mindlessly channel surfing, not really watching anything and not really spending any time with you. You know this because after a few minutes of watching something together you'll talk about what you're watching and he won't have a clue what you are talking about! The strange part for you is that if you get up and leave him to his channel surfing, he'll say: "Where are you going? I thought you wanted to spend time together!" You are completely confused because in your mind you weren't spending time together at all! So you wonder if you are growing apart because you feel lonely right next to him.

Once again, it's not what you think it is. The good news is: you are not growing apart. You are in relationship with a man and he functions much differently than you do. Let me show you why.

The Nothing Box

I've already shared with you a major problem-causing difference in his brain versus your brain: single focus. His brain is wired to think about ONE thing at a time until he's done processing that ONE thing, then he'll move on to the next thing. It's challenging, even painful to get his brain to move on to the next thing until he's finished processing the current thing. By challenging I mean it sounds like loud, confusing, angry, demanding a point or accusations of illogical trains of thought. He either becomes angry or zones out.

I've heard this brain difference between men and women described as waffles versus spaghetti.[1] A man's brain is similar to the squares on a waffle: each neat little box singularly contained, logically stacked beside each other with no two boxes touching any other boxes. Once he processes through one box he can move on to the next and the process begins again. Hence the twenty minutes it takes him to process out of work and into home that we've already talked about. In addition to that way of thinking, a man has two large boxes that are his favorite boxes. These two boxes are special because while all of the other boxes in his brain must be fully processed through before he can move onto another box, these favorites are different. He can enter into them at will, at any time, from any other box, no processing necessary.

The first box is his Sex Box. Because of the amount of testosterone flowing in a healthy man's body he can think about sex at any time. He doesn't have to process through that box before moving to another box. Many times it can be a fleeting thought. It is often triggered by anything visual. Considering the amount of sex the media uses to sell, it's easy to see how often this can be triggered. Some studies say a man thinks about sex every 52 seconds.[2] This is a reflection of the amount of testosterone flowing through his body and there is nothing wrong with him. It's actually a sign of health. What he does with those thoughts can become unhealthy, however having these thoughts in the first place is a sign of health.

The second box is the Nothing Box. Have you ever asked him,"What are you thinking about?" and received the reply: "Nothing."? He's not lying. Men are capable of thinking about nothing and it is one of their favorite brain boxes. You, however are not so fortunate. That's why you often don't believe him when he says he's thinking about nothing. But it's true, he's not holding back from you or lying to you. Your brain connects everything to everything and it's very challenging to think about nothing for long (or even short) periods of time. There are studies that show when men think about nothing, 70% of their brain activity shuts down.[3] Women just don't do that! Because of the way a man's brain focuses deeply on one thing at a time, it can be very beneficial to give the brain a break, shut down 70% of its activity and let it replenish its ability to focus deeply again. You've probably run into this "nothing box" when he's channel surfing. That's why he doesn't know what you are talking about. You've often run into the nothing box as you ask him about his feelings, or what happened at work today, or most any of the times you run into the zombie- he's in his nothing box.

This is not a rejection of you. This is not the two of you growing apart. It is the way his brain replenishes itself and it's one of his favorite brain boxes. Relax, it's not about you, it's one of his favorite boxes. The benefits of the nothing box brings something to him that is priceless and that he is after daily: peace. Many of my male clients complain that the number one thing they want when they come home after a long hard day is peace. A break from the battles of the day. But they run into a whole new slew of battles when they get home and it wreaks all kind of havoc in their lives and relationships.

Peace is mandatory to a man's life. He gets peace in his nothing box and he gets peace after sex, hence his two favorite boxes. Don't take it personally. Allow him times of peace and you will have an amazing man. Peace will refresh and refuel him so he can win the next day's battles and feel as if all the battles are worth all the cost.

Time With You

I can hear your next complaint: "Okay, Genie, so he needs peace, but why does he want me in the room when he's channel surfing? I've got things to do if he's not going to talk to me."

I'm glad you asked.

The answer is: because he **does** want to spend time with you. Spending time with you does not mean a conversation to a man. It means being together, physically in the same place. Spending time with a woman to a woman means conversation. Emmerson Eggerich the author of **Love & Respect**, calls this "shoulder to shoulder" time. For him, simply being with him, in the same room is more than enough and very satisfying. In fact, conversation can ruin it for him.

This too is a reflection of his brain chemistry. While his brain is 9% larger than yours he has a reduced number of cells in the communication and emotional areas of his brain and a larger number of cells in the spatial and focus areas of the brain compared to yours.[4]

This is one of the many reasons you want to talk more than he does, and talk in order to share emotions while he desires to talk logically. One report said you need to speak 25,000 bits of information in a day. While he needs to speak only 15,000 a day. He might have hit that while he was at work. Just because he may be out of words and in desperate need of peace doesn't mean he doesn't want to be with you. He still wants you in the room with him!

Not only that, but you have 100 times more oxytocin in your system, so your sense receptors are 10 times more sensitive to touch than his, so you feel a touch more strongly than than he does. What that means is he **needs** 3 times more touch than you do.[5] By just having you in the room he can still feel close to you, even at a time when he needs peace, not conversation or interaction. It's simply different, not wrong and not rejection.

Switzerland

Now that you understand why he's doing some of the things you thought were rejection, and now that you know they were not rejection at all, let's get you some strategies that will work with the way he's designed in order to get your needs met.

First, let's put some fun back in the relationship. Fun is vital - to both of you individually and to your relationship together if it's going to last. Life without fun is a drag, a pain, a never ending work-load that kills your spark, your inspiration and your energy. Love without fun will do the same thing to your relationship. It's crucial that you make this a priority, so much so that one of the first things I have couples do who are experiencing turmoil is go on what I call a Switzerland Date.

A Switzerland Date is a date for the two of you to do nothing but have fun together. You are not allowed to talk about anything that might cause stress, worry, difficulty, or any kind of a break in relationship. That is dealt with at another time. Switzerland is known for being neutral ground, so this date is neutral ground and only fun is discussed and had on this date. It is the priority and the only reason for the date. Once you can reconnect and have fun together you can re-ignite the spark the two of you have. So try a Switzerland Date!

Try picking something he likes and get actively involved having fun. Watch the game with him and really go for it! Yell for the team, groan at the errors, cheer and be dramatic about it. Just do it to have fun. You don't have to like it or even know what's going on. Should you choose to ask him about the rules you would be amazed at the amount of attention you'll get from him as he has an opportunity to share his expertise and excitement about the game with you.

Or try something neither of you have ever done before but have always wanted to: roller skating, biking, paddle boarding, kite flying, a board game, a picnic under the stars. Maybe you'll both find a new love you can share. If you have no ideas, watch some comedies and laugh together, it will do wonders for both of you. This is your love affair, take the time to inject it with fun again.

HA!

He knows fun is vital. He uses it to blow off steam, to reduce stress, to recharge and to enjoy life again. It's actually one of his top five needs in the relationship (it's not one of your top five needs in a relationship). That's why he makes time for it with you or without you. The only reason he would do it without you is because he might think you are no fun. It's not because he doesn't want to spend time with you. He might think you are no fun because you correct him in everything he does, because you complain, or because you don't like to do what he likes to do. Remember, each of these actions will push him away from you: correcting, complaining, or not liking what he likes.

I've developed what I call the HA! technique to help you get your needs met by your man. You can use this to get fun, to stop arguments, or even when he is trying to give you something you don't want. In fact, if you will use the HA! technique at all times, everything will get easier with him because it will meet his greatest needs as a man: honor and appreciation.

H is for Honor, A is for appreciate, and the exclamation point refers to redirecting the action. Look closely at the definitions of these words, for these words are the actions of love to him.

Honor: Dictionary.com

Noun

1.   honesty, fairness, or integrity in one's beliefs and actions

2.   a source of credit or distinction

3.   high respect, as for worth, merit, or rank

4.   high esteem; fame; glory

Verb

1.   to hold in honor or high respect; revere

2.   to treat with honor

3.   to confer honor or distinction upon

4. to accept as valid and conform to the request or demands of

Appreciation: (Dictionary.com)

Noun

1. gratitude; thankful recognition

2. the act of estimating the qualities of things and giving their proper value.

3. clear perception or recognition

You see, if you are not believing in his integrity, knowing he can handle all his decisions in life; he is not feeling loved by you. This is why questioning him can set off such a loud reaction in him- he receives your questions as disrespect and dishonoring of him. He can also see it as a lack of gratitude or recognition of all he's doing for you.

This is vitally important to understand. Because if you are not giving him credit for **all** he does for you using honor, respect and appreciation, he does not feel loved by you. If he does not feel highly respected for his worth, his accomplishments (big and small), he does not feel loved by you. Notice the last definition under verb: "to accept as valid and conform to the request or demands of," if you don't immediately conform to his requests he feels disrespected by you which is unloved!

Understanding this, you can now see that complaining is received by him as disrespect. He's not expecting you to follow his every word blindly with no opinion (although that is exactly how it can feel to you). He is expecting to be honored and respected before you begin to talk things through together. It's a small difference that makes all the difference.

Instead of complaining or arguing begin with honor for whatever it was he has done for you, or even not done for you depending upon the circumstance. You honor his intent to provide for you. It's very simple and it sounds like this: "Wow, honey you take such great care of me, thank you." After you've honored and respected him you can then add whatever it is you feel the need to add.

 Let's say he's come home and not done anything to help you and you'd like some help or some attention. That would sound like this, "You look so tired, thank you for working so hard today to take care of us." Then follow it up with appreciation: "I appreciate all you do."

Once he feels loved by you, through honor and appreciation, you can let him know exactly what help you need. Be very clear: "Honey would you please take out the trash? That would help me so much to get dinner finished." Make sure you use the word: "would," instead of the word "could." Men hear the word "could" as a capability question. Their brain responds: "Of course I have that ability." In Menglish "could" is not a request for action so he doesn't consider acting on it. The word "would" is heard as a direct request for action.

But he wants sex with you right now, he doesn't want dinner, he's not interested in taking out the trash His single focused brain is singly focused on getting you in the bedroom.   Of course sex is the last thing on your mind.   To honor and appreciate you would respond: "Yes, I want you too, but that's not going to work for me right now. I need you to take the trash out now so I can finish dinner. I would be much happier to make love to you at 10:00 tonight when I can really enjoy it."   This is the re-direct portion of the formula.   You've honored, appreciated and now you need to re-direct to get what you need. It's when you've honored and appreciated him, he can readily accept   redirection, because it's always his greatest desire to provide what you want.

The easier you make it on him to make you happy the easier it is to get your needs met because it brings him great joy to make you happy.

The biggest complaint I hear from men is: "I can't read her mind." Not only that, but they tell me they DON'T understand hints, not even obvious ones.   Seriously. They don't even notice hints. They don't think like we think, they don't want what we want and they can't figure us out. He needs you to be explicit and plain in exactly what you want and he will be more than happy to give it to you, especially if he knows ahead of time that it will make you happy.   Then simply appreciate how happy he makes you.

Fun is the answer.   It's the antidote to work, to loneliness, to stress. Bring the fun back and do it purposely and with all of your might and watch how much time he'll want to spend with you. I dare you.

Want to go deeper?

Go to:

http://www.livesuccessnow.com/more-win-influence/ for more free training, audios & videos.

Notes

1. Page 59: Laugh Your Way to a Better Marriage dvd, Mark Gungor
2. Page 60: The Female Brain, Dr. Louan Brizendine
3. Page 60: Who Switched Off My Brain? Audio Cd's Dr. Caroline Leaf
4. Page 60: Who Switched Off My Brain? Audio Cd's Dr. Caroline Leaf
5. Page 60: Who Switched Off My Brain? Audio Cd's Dr. Caroline Leaf

Chapter Twelve for Women
Influencing With Love: The Beauty

"Is this Genie Goodwin?" said the man on the other end of the phone.

"Yes, how can I help you?", I responded.

"My wife went to your **"Breakthrough"** event last weekend, what did you do to her?" he demanded.

"Why don't you tell me what you are experiencing?" I asked him.

"Well, I don't know exactly. She's not complaining at me, she's not unhappy all the time. I don't know if you know this, but we work together and she's different. She lets me talk now, about only what we're working on ,and then she drops the subject. She lets me do things without telling me how to do them, that's never...she's different. Uh. I guess the only way I know how to explain it is suddenly it's okay for me to just be a man. It's the most amazing thing."

There was silence for about thirty long seconds, then he said: "Can you help me give her the gift she's given me, can you help me do that for her?"

"Yes, I can."

This is why I do what I do. In one day everything changed for them and it only took one person knowing what to do that changed everything.

When my client originally came to me, she said things were so bad between her and her husband that she had given up on them. She said she had tried everything for years and nothing worked to make it better. She was bitter and hopeless about the relationship and looking for a way out. When I asked her what she wanted from me she said, "I have a teenage son I'm still raising, I want to make things better with him while I still can." She had given up on her marriage. That was decades of disappointment, pain and loneliness. Yet she was hoping to hang on to her son. In just one of my **Breakthrough Days** she learned simple strategies and concepts to go home and completely change her marriage and her parenting. When she did, her husband called wanting to know how he could make it better for her.

That's the amazing power of love. It transforms everything. It is the ultimate answer to anything you are struggling with in any of your relationships.

When you first start out in your love affair, he makes you feel like The Beauty, the most beautiful woman on the planet. He has chosen you, won your heart, forsaken all other women and pledged his life to yours. When he does, there is a Beauty that blossoms in you that nothing else in life can touch. His love for you changes you. You shine with it, you radiate a beauty no one has ever seen before, but now everyone can see. As his love reveals The Beauty that was always in you, your love influences him to step up to a higher level than ever before. It transforms him and reveals the Hero that has always been in him, waiting on your love to unleash him. Love inspires each of you to be magnificent and anyone around you can see it and is made better because of it.

Then you lose it, and The Beauty that influenced him to step up now nags him to be better and complains at everything he does. Your beauty is destroyed when it turns from influencing with love to nagging, from giving to selfishness. When all your words, touches and actions are aligned to change him, fix him to act more like what you want (more like a woman would act) you destroy his masculinity and kill the Hero. This is when neither of your needs for love are getting met and both of you get bitter, stressed and ugly with each other (and anyone else unfortunate enough to run into either of you). When people's' needs for love aren't met they will break their own moral standards, their own rules and beliefs, and go looking elsewhere to get their needs met. They will lie, cheat and have affairs, all of this is born from a lack of love.

Instead of fixing him, and demanding that he change to treat you better, inject the love he so desperately needs. None of us can live without love. It's like oxygen to a dying man, water to a desiccated relationship. It can bring life to a dead and bitter relationship. I've seen it turn divorced, bitter, hopeless couples back into passionate, committed, lovers who remarried. I've seen it work on children who were surly, nasty, selfish and in constant trouble. I've seen it work in offices where feuds and backbiting have taken over the company culture and made life miserable for anyone who dared enter the building. I've seen it turn alcoholics and drug addicts back into selfless, giving, caring people who contributed to others. I've seen it work over and over again in the most desperate of situations. If you think about it, you've seen love do that too.

The most miraculous thing about love is that it only takes one person to change the situation. You don't both have to be committed to change. You don't need a majority, no one even has to agree with you. It just takes you. One person walking in love can change everything.   One person walking in love becomes the most powerful person in the room. It's just that most of us haven't been taught to walk in love. We don't know how to walk it out in our day to day challenges.   We don't know what to do or say to purposely unleash it so our partner can really feel loved. We just hope it falls on us one day and hope we don't fall out of it the next day. Women have been taught to fight for our rights, that we are as good as men and we can replace men. No one is replaceable. Each of us are magnificently unique and irreplaceable. Unfortunately we are inherently selfish when we are not taught to love others.

As you read through this book you may have thought that you needed to sacrifice even more than you already are, put up with more, turn yourself into a pretzel trying to please him, ignore your needs; be the perfect wife so your man will show up again.

Don't do that.

Its much more about understanding how he works, how he was designed to work and not making him wrong for working that way. Its about understanding how you work and not making that wrong either but rather being clear on what you want and giving him an easy way to give it to you. No one is wrong, you were just created to be different. When you understand how he works and stop making him wrong for the way he does things, a miracle happens: you get to be you and he gets to be himself.

I'll tell you one more secret: the more feminine you are, the more masculinity he steps into. Its an automatic reaction in him. Don't try to be a man, don't try to fix him to act more like a woman. Just love him the way he is, in the way he can receive it and watch love do its amazing transformation in both of you.

He was made to meet your needs and you were made to meet his. In fact the more opposite you are, the more passion is created. It's your differences that create the passion. When you love each other in the way each of you can receive love, it heals all wounds and knits you two into an unbreakable, magnificent bond and life is so good.

In the last five chapters I've endeavored to share with you the top five complaints women have about men, what's really happening, and display for you how love would walk through it, and the effect love has in each of these common scenarios. I hope you've noticed the key to walking in love is always the same: stop making him wrong, understand where he's coming from and what he needs to feel loved, then give it to him.

I heard Tony Robbins say once: "You can't serve if you are judging." It has profoundly affected me and the work I do. When you make him feel loved instead of judged he will automatically respond by loving you, he doesn't even have to be trained. That's the power of love.

Congratulations on finishing this section of the book. This puts you in a rare class of people. Statistics say only 43% of the people who buy books actually finish them.[1] How many of them do you think act on what they learned? It tells me something amazing about you: your relationship is important to you and you are willing to do what it takes to create a vibrant, healthy, amazing love affair. That thought is what brought me to this place of knowing exactly what to do in any situation. To create what I call a Legendary Love Affair, a love that lasts through the years and gets deeper and more passionate the more time goes by. A love that is stronger than anything you go through.

You have an outstanding opportunity to do what it takes, sacrifice, learn, grow and keep at it until you get what you want.

The truth is when you first fell in love you did a lot of this automatically, without thinking, without training. You celebrated his differences, swooned over them. If you didn't, you wouldn't have fallen in love. If you will act that way again, the love will blossom again. This time you can do it from a place of deeper understanding. This time you can do it because you consciously know you are choosing love even when you don't feel it. That is true love. It's a choice, a commitment, a decision that is not dependent on how you feel or what he deserves. It's that level of love that unleashes amazing things in life, in you, in him, it transforms you once again into The Beauty and him into The Hero and makes the whole world better.

Remember, there is no life without love and love makes life worth living. The rewards of living this way create success and fulfillment in all aspects of your life...if you dare to walk in love.

Love is always your choice. It is always the best choice, the ultimate answer to all of the hard and challenging things we face in life. I pray you choose love, it will change your world.

Want more?

Go to:

http://www.livesuccessnow.com/more-win-influence/ for more free training, audios & videos.

Notes

1. Page 68: StatisticBrain.com

Dedication

I've added a bonus chapter for you, because love shouldn't stop when you go to work. You should love what you do and who you work with.

I believe walking in love is allowing God to lead and guide your every step, your every word, your every thought. It is caring more about the other person than you care about yourself: they are more important to you. It is creating magnificent relationships at work and at home that bring success into all facets of your life. It is the overcoming, conqueror lifestyle. It is the "how" of success and the basis for all of the work I do.

Walking In Love—-the one and only commandment that encompasses all other commandments. Yet, most people have never heard of this idea, or if they have, do not know how to do it, so they never think about it or attempt it. I believe we were created to live and operate this way, but few understand how to walk it out daily in all situations.

I met Ford Taylor in Oct. 2011 while attending his three-day Transformational Leadership seminar. I had been developing a leadership training program for companies I was working with and looking for a better way to transform relationships company-wide from the inside out than what was currently being done. I was thrilled at the concept of changing the culture of an entire company to drive profits through magnificent relationships.

Within 45 minutes of Ford's event I realized this was exactly what I had been looking for. Transformational Leadership is a series of simple tools anyone can use to transform a relationship and it has the effect of putting you in charge of what's happening in any relationship. Because you know exactly what tool to use and when to use it, it takes the mystery out of walking in love. You know I'm all about that!

I instantly became a raving fan of Ford and his work and went through the process to become one of his certified trainers. Prior to my asking, there was no formal certification program. I was part of the Portland, Oregon team, that went through the first formal program. As a certified trainer I would go on to deliver the training in a three-day event right beside Ford. It's been a great thrill of my life to do this work.

The first time he called me on stage with him, he chose the "eustress & distress" tool for me to train them in. As I got up I was nervous so I said, "This is perfect, I'm going to train you on stress and I'm experiencing high levels of it right now!" Ford laughed and stepped off stage. He told me later, "You knocked it out of the park."

At another time we were training on male and female brains, a gentleman in the audience asked the dreaded question: "What do I do when my wife asks me if she looks good in something?" I replied, "Say this: I don't know about that dress so much, but I'm crazy about the woman in it! Remember, she really wants to know you think she's beautiful, not her clothes." Ford stopped the whole event and said, "Let me write that down." That's the kind of leader he is.

Prior to my work with Ford I trained individuals, leaders and teams to walk in love through leadership training. My clients understood that no matter who they worked with, even hard to get along with individuals, they were always still in charge of their own reaction. They would always be held accountable to walk in love by me. The real secret I revealed is: if you walk in love, it will transform the other person's behavior.

Ford's program allowed me see to implementation of a new standard of relationship organization-wide. By training the entire organization in the same tools, everyone was raised to a higher standard of relationship. It took the burden off of one, while creating a team where all are supported and held accountable to healthy relationship. This is the exact model used in raising my children and the relationship standards I hold my family accountable to. It is what I have been coaching people in for years, but I had never done it organization-wide. It is exciting work to be a part of.

I believe it is the next level of transforming the way we do business, the next level of transforming the world. I respectfully dedicate this chapter, with great gratitude to Ford Taylor.

Chapter Thirteen
How to Win Her & Influence Him at Work

Do you know the one thing that will make a billionaire business owner and investor walk away from a business as if it's doomed?

Poor Relationships.

Marcus Lemonis, the CEO of Camping World & Good Sam Enterprises is worth more than $2 billion. He has expanded and currently looks for failing businesses to invest in. He says, "Distressed companies, if fixed, will yield a much higher rate of return than a well-functioning company. Higher risk, but higher reward." In order to evaluate a failing company he's preparing to invest in, he looks at three areas: the people, the process and the product.

The first area he evaluates are the people. He specifically looks at how well do the people work together? What are their strengths and weakness? Marcus says, "You can have an excellent product, and an outstandingly efficient process, but if the people relationships are poor, the business is doomed." He walks away from deals with great products and strong processes, because of people problems!

How many companies have you walked away from because of problems with people, or poor relationships? The number one reason people leave a job is because of these kinds of problems. Seventy percent of the people who leave their jobs voluntarily, leave because of their boss, not because of money.[1] When you have problems with people and relationship challenges at work, the work can be miserable, and it can become so unbearable the only answer you can think of is to leave.

When you run into these problems at work you'll experience a lack of trust in the relationship and that will infect the entire team. Back-stabbing can begin, morale will sink, absenteeism will rise, and gossip will take over the culture. People will begin covering their butt instead of their team. Large amounts of time will be spent trying to resolve problems instead of getting work done. Turnover rises, costing anywhere between 1.5 and 4 times the salary of the one who leaves. Even though most people believe the problem is over when they leave the organization, it's not true; the problem doesn't end there. Because residual bitterness will affect your new relationships, making you reluctant to trust others or you might expect to be treated the same way in your new opportunity. Efficiency levels go down, deadlines on projects are missed, and you are miserable as the stress gets higher and higher. You can't sleep, you can't relax, it begins to affect all of your relationships in life because you are struggling to find a way through it. You come home stressed and take it out on your loved ones even though you don't mean to.

If you are angry at work, you actually lose creativity and wisdom. Anger shuts off the parts of your brain that can logically think through things and can also shut down your creativity so its harder to find answers.[1] With strained relationships and lower creativity, your focus goes down, and the quality of your work absolutely suffers. Does any of this cost you money? You bet it does, more money than you've ever considered. But it cost so much more than money. That's why people quit. It's a huge problem.

But what if what you think is a people problem, is actually a reflection of male/female dynamics? You've already discovered in this book that men and women communicate differently, they also work differently. By understanding how the masculine works and working with men instead of blocking them, and understanding how the feminine works and supporting women the way they need to be supported instead of expecting them to act like men, you can obliterate so many of the relationship problems we run into. Then both men and women can make a difference in this world, working together, side by side. We work much better together than we do apart.

"My new boss is a jerk! I've been training to become a manager in the corporation. While my training was going on it was decided that they would bring in an outside hire as the interim manager. He hadn't been trained in company policy. He didn't know the standards or protocols of the company. I was doing my best to help him get acclimated into the company but he would have nothing to do with anything I had to say. He regularly cut me off when I

tried to explain company policy. He'd say things like: "Well that's not the way we are doing it now." He seemed like a bully to me. He wouldn't even listen to a full sentence. He was offending team members and they were coming to me to complain. He rudely interrupted people when they talked. He would give orders he expected to be followed and it didn't matter in the least to him that it was not company policy or the way we did things. I've tried hard to support him, but it seems like he's more interested in doing things his way than in creating a team. The more I try, the worse it gets. Now it seems to me like he is determined to get rid of me. I don't know what to do to work with him. I love this company, but working with him is a nightmare."

My client ran into relationship problems at work and it was making her life miserable. It was a hard spot to be in and she had run out of answers when she contacted me.

Many of the problems at work are actually male/female dynamics at play. That was definitely going on for my client. In this case, she needed to understand first how a man accomplishes goals, and then what in particular he was trying to accomplish. Only then could she support him in the way he would receive her support. Only then could they work together so they could both shine.

She wanted to support him but without understanding how to influence a man at work it seemed to her like the more she tried, the worse he got. It was a simple misunderstanding of the way men and women work. With a few tweaks in the way she interacted with him, he could become her greatest support.

How a Man Works

The first thing she needed to understand is how men work.   At work a man's number one priority is to establish his authority and expertise. As a leader, it becomes even more important that he not only establish his expertise, but he must also achieve his objectives at all costs.   He takes this responsibility seriously, so he will focus primarily on results. From this position of achieving results he will begin to launch his objectives.   With his single-focused brain he will focus on his objectives above all else. That means anything that slows down his progress will be seen as a problem.   He will focus on evidence of achieving his outcomes: numbers, finding anything measurable: charts, graphs, or any results that can establish his authority.   This is the way a male runs a business, and it's not conducive to the way a female operates. Because as he focuses on his objectives, when his subordinate question his decisions, he can typically consider that as either disrespectful; or a challenge to his authority and expertise. His reaction will be to stop whatever he believes that is and re-establish his authority. This is exactly what she was going through. However, not understanding it, she took it personally, as if he had it out for her. He didn't. He was simply trying to achieve his objectives and anything she did that wasn't in alignment with that, was in his way, it wasn't personal to him at all, it was objective driven.

You see, a female leader will be more concerned with creating relationships that build team in order to achieve the objectives. She will accomplish the results, but her tendency is to do work through team instead of achieving by herself. The feminine will try to build community so the work gets done by the team, not by a superstar. You can see this male/female dynamic show up in many meetings: she will poll the team for ideas and feedback, making sure everyone is heard and contributing. Whereas he will announce what the objectives are and expect people to go get the work done on their own, as quickly as possible, without involving others. This is because the masculine prefers to work alone, while the feminine prefers to work in groups.

Her Number One Tool In Working With a Man

Knowing how a man works, I began to train my client how to support him more suitably in the ways he would accept. This allows him to work seamlessly with her while cutting the stress for both of them. It was a simple change. Her number one tool would be respect.

Respect honors him and his expertise, allowing him to hear what she has to say, without his having to fight her to establish his position.

When she needed to question him, instead of using the feminine strategy of directly questioning, which would inevitably make him cut her off in reaction to his perceived disrespect, I gave her some strategies that would meet his need for respect and get her answers easily.

 She was to use these specific words: "I know you have a reason for what you are doing, would you explain it to me?" This simple phrase establishes his authority and shows respect which makes him willing to share details with her. She didn't have to agree with him, she simply needed to show him respect. It's the words: "I know you have a reason," that he receives as respect. Once he felt respected he was more open to giving her the time she needed to understand the details behind his objectives so she could fully support him.

If she had a comment, a thought or an idea she wanted to offer, but he hadn't asked her for input, his unconscious reaction, due to her phrasing, would be to feel immediately challenged or disrespected. This is when he would cut her off, order her to do things, or simply demand something be done. These reactions revealed his perceived lack of respect. When he was in achievement mode, and had not asked for her input, and her response was, "That's not the way the company does it," her input was interpreted by him as disrespect. He would then respond: "Well that's the way we do it now." She began to take that personal and it caused even more friction in the office. Another useful phrase I recommended when she wanted to offer her ideas that weren't invited was: "You probably already know this, but just in case"...then she could add her comment without him reacting as if he was being challenged or disrespected. This would open up dialog for each of them to bring their talents into play without either one being hurt or disrespected or escalating stress in the relationship.

If she disagreed with something he was doing the strategy could be to say: "I respectfully disagree," then she could add why and he could more easily hear it and they could then work it out together. She could even cut him off as he was talking with a "I respectfully disagree" and it wouldn't be a problem. Most men have no problem with disagreement, their problem and harsh response is in reaction to perceived disrespect, not in being interrupted or disagreed with.

By adding respect to her conversation in the way a man receives respect, she made it much easier for him to work with her, rather than fighting her to get his work done. It's a simple change that makes all the difference in the world, because men run on respect. Once he perceives he is respected he will be much more interested in having the detailed conversations she needs to work with him.

His Number One Tool
In Working With a Woman

If I were coaching him instead of her for this situation, I would have equipped him with the most powerful tool in working with a woman: conversation. The feminine at work is relationship oriented, as opposed to the male task orientation. Notice, it really is opposed orientations, and it feels that way when you try to work together without understanding each other. She needs to be heard and understood to create the healthiest work environment. It is through being heard she feels the connection of relationship that allows her to work excellently. In his desire to perform well, he was unknowingly undermining this. Its not important that he always agree with her, it's simply important that she be heard. By not allowing her open communication he was unaware of the great amount of stress he was causing her, while making it very hard for her to support him or his initiatives.

Unfortunately, because the masculine is so task oriented, men often believe if she's talking about something instead of doing it, she must not be capable of doing it. Once he thinks that, he loses respect for her simply because she's talking about it. This is a dangerous error in judgement because it is rarely true.

The feminine uses conversation to build support for her strategy, while the masculine prefers to develop his strategy quietly on his own. This male method of working can damage relationship in the mind of a woman, because it creates autonomy instead of community. She experiences this as being cut off, disregarded, unappreciated, and she'll begin to think he is egotistical, or selfish, which all makes for a bad work relationship. He thinks she's incapable and she thinks he's a jerk to work with, it's a typical misunderstanding, and very unfortunate.

The feminine drive to build community, by creating deep and solid relationships with your customers and your team members is what builds sustained businesses and higher profits. She does most of the relationship building with conversation. The business world needs problem solvers and relationship builders side by side instead of judging each other. Having strong relationships and innovative achievement is a winning combination.

Men at work use conversation for basically one reason: fix it. Women use conversation for four reasons, according to Dr. John Gray in his book: *How to Get What You Want at Work*. The four reasons are: convey content, inform of her emotional state, relieve tension, and to create clarity and discover a solution. By not allowing her to talk he basically cut off her ability to process.

Knowing she has four uses for conversation, he simply needs to respect her range and adeptness with which she uses conversation rather than stopping conversation so he could achieve on his own. The simplest solution is to ask her if she has any questions or comments, then listen to her response without interrupting. If he disagrees with her, he could simply say, "I hear you, thanks for sharing that, but we are doing it this way. I'd appreciate your support."

If he truly didn't have the time to listen to her comments he could offer to talk with her at the end of the day. Simply offering to take the time later will be well received and make her feel supported. It's also fine to let her know you only have a minute but you want to hear what she has to say, let her know when the time is up and thank her for her input. Gratitude goes a long way in creating healthy relationships.

"Thanks for sharing" is a great response no matter what she has used conversation for. If she's upset he could ask: "Are you just blowing off steam?" Or "Do you need to blow off some steam?" She will take this as hugely supportive and a deep relationship strengthener. You can even say, "I think you need to blow off some steam, I've got 3 minutes for you, let 'er rip." That way she feels supported without it taking more time than you have available.

If he is confused by her conversation: "Sounds like you're working on it, do you need anything from me?" is a great clarifier. Understand, it's important to give her time for conversation, but it doesn't have to take large amounts of time, simply small, daily conversations where she feels heard will make all the difference. For extra points, adding a "how's your family" will be invaluable to creating a strong relationship with a woman. It's an investment that will pay off hugely for the relationship and the business.

Male vs. Female Stress!

The second thing to understand is the difference in the way men and women experience stress. In the story of my client's new boss he was feeling pressure to perform. Each member of his new team was also feeling stressed, wanting to make a good impression on him. That's a recipe for stress at work. When a man is under stress to achieve something he will pull away from others to focus on his goals and achieve them. Typically while under stress he may grumble, scowl, and mumble as he processes his answers. Women tend to take this personally, as if he doesn't like her. That's not what is happening, it's not personal to him at all. It's just the masculine noises of stress.

When a woman is under stress she will complain, whine and try to talk it all through in order to process it. The more she talks, the better she feels because she is resolving issues in her life; and everything is personal to the feminine. When she is listened to, especially when she is sharing vulnerable feelings, with sympathy or empathy, she feels the most supported. Therefore, if she can't talk it through it becomes much more difficult to solve.

When he won't talk about it, she becomes more stressed. However, the more she talks, the more stress he experiences because he can't focus on getting his objectives done. He wants to get right to the solution and achieve, because he is achievement oriented. She wants to be heard and understood before performing, because she is relationship oriented. Stress makes him want to focus even more on achievement, while it makes her want to focus even more on relationships. This pulls the two of them in opposite directions as they are trying to achieve the same goal!

The simple solution for her is to talk it through with someone else who would listen without judgement or comment. Preferably someone not in the office or a part of the organization, to prevent gossip. Gossip causes great damage in an organization and should be avoided at all times. If she felt the need to talk to him, she could achieve that by simply letting him know she was frustrated and needed to vent with him for ten minutes. This would solve it so she could focus on achieving their objectives again. That put him in the position where he clearly knew the time spent would help them achieve the objectives instead of being wasted. Then he is much more interested in helping in a way that is acceptable to her.

When he is stressed, getting his mind off of it and doing something physical is a great stress buster for a man. Running, sports, a drive, watching a game, anything that allows his brain to stop focusing on the stress and get a break helps him to overcome stress and come back refreshed, ready to fix it.

What looked like a bad fit was actually a function of male/female dynamics: what he needed to be able to work well and what she needed to be able to work well. It is the difference between how the masculine works and how the feminine. Unfortunately, if male/female dynamics are ignored, the relationship challenges can be too much to get through. In this particular case she was not able to make the changes fast enough and he let her go. We found out shortly thereafter that he was also let go. She lost, he lost and the company lost because they didn't have the skills to master the relationship problems. It doesn't have to be this way.

Understanding the needs of men and women at work and delivering it in the way each can receive, makes the difference between profit and loss. It also makes the difference between stress and fulfillment, between work and hell. When men and women can work together, side by side, each providing their particular strengths, businesses prosper and lives are bettered.

Want more?

Go to: http://www.livesuccessnow.com/more-win-influence/ for more training, audios & videos.

Notes

1. Page 73: Assocham study quoted on 9inchmarketing.com

2. Page 74: Who Switched Off My Brain? Dr. Caroline Leaf